Ribambelle—French slang for a group of kids—in Le Chambon, winter 1943-1944. Jean (see Chapter Sixteen, "In the Maquis: Jean") is at the far right. His sister, Anne-Marie, is sixth from left. Rudi (see Chapter Six, "Lighting Hanukkah Candles: Rudi") is fifth from right.

HIDDEN

ON THE

Mountain

Stories of Children
Sheltered from the Nazis
in Le Chambon

DEBORAH DURLAND DESAIX

KAREN GRAY RUELLE

HOLIDAY HOUSE | NEW YORK

Text copyright © 2007 by Deborah Durland DeSaix and Karen Gray Ruelle
All Rights Reserved
Book design by Maura Fadden Rosenthal/Mspace
Maps on pages xiii–xvii by Heather Saunders
Printed in the United States of America
www.holidayhouse.com
First Edition
1   3   5   7   9   10   8   6   4   2

Library of Congress Cataloging-in-Publication Data
Ruelle, Karen Gray.
Hidden on the mountain : stories of children sheltered from the Nazis in le Chambon /
by Karen Gray Ruelle and Deborah Durland Desaix.— 1st ed.
p. cm.
Includes bibliographical references and index.
ISBN-13: 978-0-8234-1928-9 (hardcover)
ISBN-10: 0-8234-1928-2 (hardcover)
1. Jewish children in the Holocaust—France—Le Chambon-sur-Lignon—Biography—
Juvenile literature. 2. Holocaust, Jewish (1939-1945)—France—Le Chambon-sur-
Lignon—Personal narratives—Juvenile literature. 3. World War, 1939-1945—
Jews—Biography—Juvenile literature. 4. Le Chambon-sur-Lignon (France)—Ethnic
relations—Juvenile literature. I. DeSaix, Deborah Durland. II. Title.
DS135.F89R84 2007
940.53'18092244595—dc22
2006002033

We dedicate this book to the people of Le Chambon
and all of La Montagne Protestante,
in admiration of their indomitable spirit.

CONTENTS

NOTE TO READERS

THESE ARE THE STORIES of children and teenagers who lived in a particular time and place—Jewish refugees who had to flee their homes during World War II, and young people in the haven that those refugees found in and around Le Chambon-sur-Lignon, in southern France.

We first learned of Le Chambon during a visit to France in 2002. In a tiny museum in the center of town, a local historian told us the dramatic story of rescue and refuge that had taken place there. The courageous farmers and villagers of this sparsely inhabited region defied the Nazis by saving the lives of thousands of innocent Jews, most of them children. Awed and moved, we decided that we had to tell this story to others. We were surprised to discover that no one had written a nonfiction book for children about Le Chambon.

History comes alive when it is related by those who have lived it. We were determined to find Jews who, as children, had found refuge in Le Chambon during the war. We would interview them and tell the story through their eyes. A collection of their real-life experiences would illuminate many facets of this amazing story, and we could fill in the rest with supporting chapters based on our research. Even though we had never written this kind of book before, we felt compelled to try. It was now or never. The children whose lives had been saved in Le Chambon were in their seventies or older, and most of their rescuers had already passed away. Their stories were in danger of disappearing. And so we rushed headlong into the project; we had no idea what we were getting into!

It wasn't easy tracking down people who had been rescued in Le Chambon. After the war they had scattered, and now they could be living anywhere in the world. We began our research at the library, and we checked the Internet. One of the references we turned up was the documentary film about Le Chambon, *Weapons of the*

Spirit. We contacted the director of the film and he put us in touch with some people, who in their turn led us to others. We also pursued leads we discovered in the many reference and history books we read. We searched online and even used phone books. Eventually, we managed to locate and contact thirty people—former refugees, rescuers, Resistance fighters, historians, and others.

We couldn't expect these people to come to us to tell their stories, yet we wanted to speak with them in person, not over the phone. We hoped that by meeting face-to-face we would learn more about them as we asked our questions and they told us their stories. In addition, we felt that sitting and talking together would make it easier for them as they recounted decades-old memories of what were often traumatic experiences. Armed with our tape recorders—and it's a good thing we brought along two, because during an interview one of our tape recorders broke mid-sentence—we traveled to New York, Florida, and Virginia to talk to people in their homes. Many of our interviewees still lived in France. Some spoke no English. Fortunately, both of us speak French. We traveled all over France and conducted most of those interviews in French. We even drove to Switzerland for the afternoon in order to interview one person. We found that many of the stories intersected with one another, and some people who became friends at that time remain friends to this day. Of the people we spoke with, some had never told their story before. Others had told their story often, to school groups or for oral history archives. One person said that he would only tell his story to us, and never again—once was enough.

The road up into the mountains toward Le Chambon is winding and steep, and then the landscape flattens into gentler hills as you reach the high plateau. We spent days exploring the village and the surrounding area. We saw some of the actual farms and children's homes where young refugees had been sheltered, and we met with local historians and people who had grown up alongside the refugees. Our hotel had been a boardinghouse during the war. As we climbed the stairs to our rooms, we imagined we could hear the clatter of *sabots*—wooden clogs—worn by the children who had been sheltered in that very building.

We were both nervous and excited as we met with each new person. It was difficult to be a witness as they relived wrenching emotional moments. At the same time, it was thrilling to hear history recounted firsthand. They graciously welcomed us into their homes, showing us precious memorabilia and offering us delicious home-cooked treats. As they talked to us about their childhood experiences, their faces often reflected the pain and loss they had suffered. At other times, they smiled as they remembered old friends and youthful escapades. Most of the interviews were hours long, and we left feeling exhilarated and exhausted. Afterward, as we thought about what the former refugees had told us, we often felt an overwhelming sadness about what they had been through.

We are children's book writers, but we are not professional interviewers or historians. We prepared carefully and learned quickly. Although our interviews contained a wealth of detail and information, they were not chronological or ordered, and often the information was fragmented. We couldn't simply include the interviews in the book as they were, because they wouldn't make any sense. We needed to reformat them. First-person accounts are exciting; they bring the reader right into the moment. So we chose to keep these accounts in the first person, as they were told. We did modify the verb tenses, as if each person were narrating events as they happened. We made nothing up—everything we wrote comes directly from what our interviewees told us, how they told it to us, and other personal accounts (autobiographical writings, videotaped oral histories, and diaries). All events and conversations we describe actually took place, according to the people we interviewed. We invented no dialogue. All dialogue or words in quotation marks we have included verbatim from our interviews (translated into English when necessary). When we ascribed emotional responses to a young refugee, these were always feelings that the person had described to us. Each person checked his or her chapter for accuracy and approved it. Only four people did not check their chapters. Two of them did not speak English well enough, the third chose not to, and the fourth passed away before her chapter was finished. In that case, her widower checked her chapter and approved it. We firmly believe we have captured each personality and his or her story truthfully.

In two cases, however, we were not able to conduct an interview ourselves with a former refugee, so we wrote chapters based on written accounts they sent us. These chapters did not have the details necessary for a first-person narrative, therefore we wrote their stories in the third person. Also, when the narrator would have been too young to tell his or her story directly, we wrote in the third person.

We included chapters touching on the lives of other young people in Le Chambon, in order to create a complete picture of what life was like there. These portraits are more brief and are all told in the third person. Because they were not Jewish refugees, their stories are not the main focus of the book. For the chapters about the rescuers, a great deal of our information came from their own written testimonies. We were sorry that we didn't have the chance to speak with them before they passed away.

If there are any errors of fact in our book, the fault lies with us, or perhaps with the nature of memory. Memories are colored by feelings and impressions, and filtered through time. Sometimes two people will remember the same event differently, and each memory feels true and exact to each of them. In every biographical chapter, we've told the story as it was remembered by the person with whom we spoke. When a first-person testimony was in conflict with another historical source, we've chosen to go with the former.

Researching and writing the story of Le Chambon and the people who found refuge there has been an amazing journey of nearly four years. We've made new friends and traveled new roads. Our lives have been made richer by the experience. It is our hope that this book will allow you, our reader, to see life through the eyes of these brave young Jewish refugees.

—Debora Durland DeSaix and
Karen Gray Ruelle

EUROPE DURING WORLD WAR II

Nazi concentration camp

⊗ Nazi death camp

area under Nazi control during the war

N

IRELAND
SCOTLAND
WALES
ENGLAND

North Sea

NORWAY
SWEDEN
FINLAND

DENMARK
Baltic Sea

ESTONIA
LATVIA
LITHUANIA
KALININGRAD

Atlantic Ocean

English Channel

Rotterdam
Brussels
Antwerp
HOLLAND
BELGIUM

Bergen-Belsen
Berlin
GERMANY
Frankfurt
Wurzburg
Mannheim
Nuremburg

Ravensbrück
Treblinka
Warsaw
POLAND
Maidanek
Auschwitz

SOVIET UNION

(only a portion of the Soviet Union was controlled by the Nazis)

Paris
LUXEMBOURG
Saarland
Karlsruhe

FRANCE

Besançon
Basel
SWITZERLAND
Geneva

Le Chambon

Dachau

CZECHOSLOVAKIA

Vienna
AUSTRIA
HUNGARY

ROMANIA

YUGOSLAVIA

BULGARIA

PORTUGAL
Lisbon
SPAIN

Corsica

Sardinia

ITALY

Adriatic Sea

ALBANIA
GREECE

Mediterranean Sea

Sicily

AFRICA

FRANCE UNDER NAZI OCCUPATION

principal French
internment camp

BELGIUM

GERMANY

LUXEMBOURG

English Channel

Northern
(Occupied)
Zone

Drancy
Paris

Atlantic
Ocean

DEMARCATION   LINE

ALPS

SWITZERLAND

Lake Leman

Vichy

Annemasse

Villeurbanne
Lyon

Annecy

St. Etienne

Grenoble

Southern
(Unoccupied)
Zone

Le Puy

Le Chambon

ITALY

Italian Zone
(November 1942–
September 1943)

Agen

Figeac

Condom

Toulouse

Montpellier

Les Milles

Auch

Marseille

Gurs

Le Vernet

Rivesaltes

SPAIN

St. Cyprien

Mediterranean   Sea

LA MONTANGE PROTESTANTE DURING WORLD WAR II

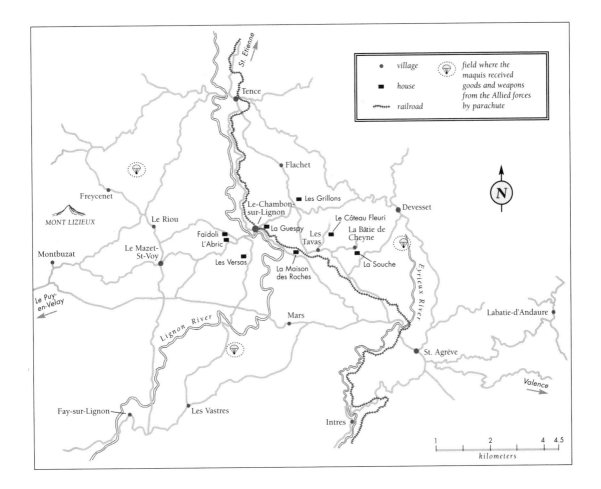

TIME LINE

January 30, 1933	Adolf Hitler becomes chancellor of Germany
February 28, 1933	Hitler is granted emergency powers
March 23, 1933	"Enabling Act" gives the Nazi government dictatorial power
April 1, 1933	First boycott of Jewish businesses in Germany
April 7, 1933	"Aryan Law" passed in Germany banning Jews and other non-Aryans from working for the government and as lawyers
September 22, 1933	German Jews no longer allowed to work as journalists, artists, writers, and musicians, or to work in broadcasting or the theater
September 29, 1933	Jews in Germany forbidden to own land or to be farmers
August 2, 1934	Hitler proclaims himself *führer*—he is now the dictator of Germany
January 1937	German Jews banned from working in most professions
March 12, 1938	Germany takes over Austria
November 9–10, 1938	*Kristallnacht*—The Night of Broken Glass—was a time of violence against Jews all over Germany
March 15, 1939	German troops occupy Czechoslovakia
September 1, 1939	Germany invades Poland
September 3, 1939	Britain and France declare war on Germany—World War II begins
May 10, 1940	Germany invades the Netherlands, Belgium, Luxembourg, and France
May 15, 1940	The Netherlands surrenders to Germany

May 20, 1940	Nazis open Auschwitz, a concentration camp in Poland
May 28, 1940	Belgium surrenders to Germany
June 10, 1940	Italy enters the war on Germany's side
June 14, 1940	The first inmates arrive at Auschwitz
June 22, 1940	France surrenders to Germany
July 11, 1940	Collaborationist Vichy government formed in France
July 17, 1940	Vichy puts its first anti-Semitic regulation in place
June 22, 1941	Germany invades the Soviet Union
July 1941	Elisabeth arrives in Le Chambon—works and lives at Pastor Trocmé's house
September 1, 1941	Jews in Germany have to wear a yellow Star of David
September 1941	Joseph, Jakob, and Hanne all come to Le Chambon— they live at La Guespy
December 7, 1941	Elisabeth and her family cross the border into Spain
February 1942	First use at Auschwitz of poison gas to kill large numbers of Jews at a time.
March 27, 1942	First convoy of Jews deported from France to Auschwitz
May 29, 1942	Vichy enacts laws forbidding Jews to go to all restaurants, cafés, libraries, sporting events, parks, and other public places
June 7, 1942	Vichy mandates that all Jews in France must wear a yellow Star of David
June 15, 1942	Vichy suggests to the Nazis that Jewish children as young as two years old be deported from France
June 1942	Lise comes to Le Chambon—stays at Tante Soly
July 16–17, 1942	More than 12,880 Jews, including about 4,000 children, are arrested in Paris—the largest single roundup of Jews in France

July 1942	Nathalie arrives in Le Chambon—stays at L'Abric Renée arrives in Le Chambon—stays on the Fourniers' farm
August 1942	Max arrives in Le Chambon—is hidden by farmers
September 1942	Rudi arrives in Le Chambon—stays at La Guespy Max crosses the border into Switzerland
October 1, 1942	Renée, with her family, crosses the border into Switzerland
November 11, 1942	Germans occupy the Southern Zone of France
January 17, 1943	Peter arrives in Le Chambon—stays at Les Grillons
Winter 1943	Erna comes to Le Chambon—lives and works at L'Abric Claude arrives on the plateau—lives on the Ollivier farm
February 28, 1943	Hanne crosses the border into Switzerland
April 1943	Jakob crosses the border into Switzerland
July 1943	Henri comes to Le Chambon—stays at Faïdoli
September 8, 1943	Italy surrenders to the Allies
May 22, 1944	Peter crosses the border into Switzerland
June 6, 1944	D-Day—Allied forces invade occupied France
August 22, 1944	Last convoy of Jews deported from France to Auschwitz
August 25, 1944	Allied army liberates Paris
September 3, 1944	French army arrives in Le Chambon-sur-Lignon—Liberation!—Rudi, Nathalie, Joseph, Lise, and Claude are still living on the plateau
January 27, 1945	Soviet army liberates Auschwitz
April 30, 1945	Hitler commits suicide in Berlin
May 7, 1945	Germany surrenders unconditionally to the Allies—the war is over in Europe, and V-E Day (Victory in Europe Day) is celebrated the next day

PROLOGUE

IMAGINE HAVING TO LEAVE your home suddenly, with only one small suitcase and no more. Imagine being told that you can't say good-bye to your friends, and that you have to leave behind your pets and all of your treasured possessions. Imagine walking out of your home, not knowing if you'll ever see it again.

Now imagine that your parents are more frightened than you've ever seen them before. You've seen terrible things, and you're frightened, too. Imagine that your parents are powerless to protect you or even themselves.

Maybe you and your family have to board a train, along with huge crowds of other people, and travel far away. Or maybe your family has been torn from you and you are all alone. You have no idea where to go or what will happen next.

Many children in Europe had just these experiences during the World War II. Many of them died. But some children were lucky, and they found a safe place to hide while the war raged on around them. Several thousand children were sheltered in the little village of Le Chambon-sur-Lignon and the surrounding area in southern France. In this book, we tell the true stories of some of these children. Each one came to Le Chambon on a different path from a different place. Each one found a safe haven among the inhabitants of the plateau. Each one has a different story.

HIDDEN
ON THE
Mountain

Hitler climbs the stairs at a huge Nazi meeting in 1934. The swastika on the banners, an ancient symbol, was used by the Nazis as their official emblem.

CHAPTER ONE.

War!
World War II
Begins

IN THE YEAR 1940, Jews in Europe were in grave danger. Germany was invading country after country, and Adolf Hitler, Germany's chancellor, hated Jews. His eventual plan was to murder Europe's entire Jewish population in what he called "The Final Solution of the Jewish Question." By 1945, as a result of this hatred, six million Jews had died in what is known as the Holocaust.

Hitler, head of the Nazi party, became chancellor in 1933. For several years prior to that, Germany had been facing terrible problems—factories had been forced to cut their production almost in half, and by January 1933, nearly one-third of the population was out of work. People were hungry and desperate, and Hitler promised to make the country great again. It was easy for Hitler to blame the Jews for Germany's problems. For centuries, Jews had been treated as scapegoats in Europe,

Hitler gives the Nazi salute to ranks of young Germans during a parade in Nürnberg in 1935.

and anti-Semitism—hatred of Jews—was common. Hitler referred to Jews as maggots, parasites, vermin, vampires, and snakes. Nazis proclaimed that Jews were a filthy disease that had to be wiped out.

Nazis believed that Jews were not simply people of another religion but actually a different race. Hitler said that the German race must be "pure" and free of Jewish influence. This superior Germanic race was called Aryan. It was based on the typical northern European's appearance: tall, blond, and blue-eyed.

Jews were not the only ones thought to be inferior. Nazis also despised Slavs, Gypsies, Jehovah's Witnesses, homosexuals, criminals, the mentally ill, people with physical deformities or handicaps, and anyone who didn't look Aryan. However, Jews were especially singled out.

As soon as Hitler became chancellor, he began taking action against Jews. Starting with a boycott of Jewish businesses, his government went on to pass hundreds of laws against the Jews. The laws forbade Jews to work in almost all professions, to own homes, to attend public schools, to shop in non-Jewish stores, to go to movies or theaters, to own radios, to travel, or even to leave home in the evening.

On November 9–10, 1938, Nazis went on a rampage throughout Germany, destroying Jewish homes and stores, beating and arresting Jewish men, and desecrating and setting fire to nearly every synagogue, all while firemen and police stood by doing nothing. Because of all the windows that were shattered, this horrific event is now known as Kristallnacht—the Night of Broken Glass.

Eventually, Jews were required to wear a yellow Star of David attached to their clothing whenever they went out, to show that they were Jewish. Many Jews were humiliated and attacked every day.

The Nazis invaded Poland in 1939. France and Britain declared war on Germany in response, and World War II began. Poland fell to the Nazis in less than a month. Germany had already taken over Austria and Czechoslovakia. By the summer of 1940, the Nazis had conquered Denmark, Norway, Belgium, Luxembourg, the Netherlands, and France. The Nazis brought their hatred of Jews with them everywhere they went. European Jews had fewer and fewer places where they could be safe.

German troops march into Warsaw, Poland, on October 5, 1939, shortly after Poland's defeat.

A Frenchman cries as he watches German soldiers marching down the streets of Paris on June 14, 1940.

CHAPTER TWO

Collaborating with the Nazis
Vichy France

AFTER FRANCE SURRENDERED TO GERMANY in June 1940, the country was divided into two zones. The demarcation line that separated the two zones was like a border between two countries. The line was guarded, and no one could cross it without a special pass.

The northern part of the country was directly controlled by the Nazis. It was called the Occupied Zone. The Unoccupied Zone was in the south, ruled by a new French government. Led by Maréchal (Marshal) Philippe Pétain, the Vichy government, headquartered in the city of Vichy, had agreed to cooperate with Germany. Pétain's anti-Semitic government immediately began to pass anti-Jewish laws that became even more cruel than those of the Nazis.

Before France fell, many Jews had fled to France from other countries to escape

Jewish refugee children from Germany arrive in France by train
sometime between 1933 and 1936.

the Nazis. Others had come to France after being forced out of Germany. This
meant that France had a large number of foreign-born Jews. Now they were especially at risk and could be arrested at any time.

France had already created a number of internment camps—places that were
like prison camps. They were originally set up to house refugees from the Spanish
Civil War. Now these camps were being used to imprison Jewish men, women, and

A Nazi exhibition in Paris in 1941, *Le Juif et la France*—The Jew and France—portrayed Jews as evil subhumans who wished to destroy France. About one hundred thousand Parisians saw this exhibition in its first few days.

children. The camps were overcrowded and horrendous. Hot in the summer and cold in the winter, there was very little heat and no hot water. The bathrooms were often big open pits dug in the ground. It was impossible to stay clean. There was no privacy. There was never enough food, and there were rats, lice, fleas, and bedbugs. Illnesses spread quickly. Many people in the camps died of starvation and disease.

The *gendarmes*—French police—would sometimes round up and arrest hundreds or even thousands of Jews at a time and send them to these internment camps. The largest roundup took place in Paris in the summer of 1942. About thirteen thousand Jews, including four thousand children, were herded into the Vel d'Hiv sports stadium. They were held there for days without food or water, before being taken away to the Drancy transit camp.

Drancy was the last stop for many Jews before being sent out of France. As part of Hitler's Final Solution for the Jews, death camps were created in Poland. The death camps were far worse than France's internment camps. Their sole purpose was to kill Jews. One of the death camps, Auschwitz, was the final destination for almost everyone who was sent to Drancy.

These babies are in the Gurs internment camp, where they were born.

These children were left, orphaned, in the Rivesaltes internment camp after their parents had been deported.

Sometimes Jewish mothers were arrested with their babies and young children. One of the more cruel actions of the Vichy government was the practice of separating mothers from their children in the internment camps. The mothers were sent away to Drancy, and then Auschwitz, torn from their young ones and forced to leave them behind. Eventually these babies and children were sent away in crowded cattle cars to meet the same fate as their mothers.

The Vichy government sent 75,700 Jews to death camps. Of that number, 11,402 were children, many of them under the age of six. Of all the children deported, only about three hundred survived. All the others perished.

Prisoners at Drancy wash while armed French guards look on. The men, women, and children held in Drancy had little or no privacy when washing or using the latrine.

Le Chambon-sur-Lignon, as seen from across the Lignon River

CHAPTER THREE

An Isolated Haven
Le Chambon-sur-Lignon and La Montagne Protestante

SEVERAL HUNDRED YEARS AGO in France, another group of people needed a safe place. This group needed somewhere they could live without fear of persecution. These people, Huguenot Protestants, were living in a Catholic country, where they had been arrested, tortured, and even killed because of their religion.

Many Huguenots left the country, but some hid in different areas of France. Some lived in an area that became known as La Montagne Protestante—The Protestant Mountain. It is an isolated mountainous plateau in south-central France. Few people lived there. The winters were very harsh. The Huguenots continued to suffer terrible persecution for many years, even in this isolated spot. They held their religious services in secret, often in the woods up on the slopes of Mont Lizieux, an extinct volcano that dominates the landscape. Eventually they were able to practice their religion

In winter, deep snowfalls could cut off the people of La Montagne Protestante from the outside world.

openly and live there in peace. But they never forgot how it felt to be persecuted.

Fiercely independent, the Huguenot Protestants had a strong sense of right and wrong. They valued their own freedom and respected the freedom of others. They were modest and humble. They believed in tolerance and in sharing what they had with others. Every day they read the Bible, and they were committed to living their lives according to what they read. They didn't blindly accept the authority of the government if it contradicted their religious beliefs.

Protestants have always been a very small minority in France. Most people in France are Catholic. In 1940 less than 1 percent of the entire population was Protestant. However, Protestants of all types, including the descendants of the Huguenots, made up ninety percent of the people who lived on the farms and in the villages scattered across La Montagne Protestante.

Les Versas, the farm on the plateau where Léon and Marthe (*see* Chapter Twelve, "Spies Next Door: Léon and Marthe"), natives of Le Chambon, grew up

Le Chambon-sur-Lignon is the largest of twelve small villages up on this mountainous plateau. At the time of the war, more than half of the people who lived there were farmers and peasants. The farms were small and tucked in among the trees and hills. Some were in clusters of three or four. Others were quite isolated, far from any neighbors. A farm might have several cows and perhaps a few goats, pigs, rabbits, or chickens. If a farmer had as many as five cows, he would be considered wealthy! The rocky soil was poor, only good for growing certain crops. The farmers grew things like rye, potatoes, cabbages, leeks, and carrots.

The people of La Montagne Protestante had a centuries-long history of welcoming those in need. In 1893, they began taking in poor city children to spend the summer in the healthy mountain air. The children stayed on farms or in *pensions*—boardinghouses—and entire families came to vacation there as well. During the Spanish Civil War in the 1930s, many Spanish refugees came to stay. It was a region that was accustomed to welcoming strangers.

Now there was another war going on. In 1940, in divided France, La Montagne Protestante was in the southern Unoccupied Zone. Refugees from the north of France and from other countries had been fleeing the Nazis since Hitler came to power. The persecution that the Jews were suffering reminded the French Protestants of the suffering and persecution of their own Huguenot ancestors. The treatment of the Jews by the Nazis and the Vichy government went against everything their religion had taught them.

In fact, Protestants of La Montagne Protestante felt a special bond with Jews, as the chosen people of the Bible, and they accepted the Jewish roots of their own religion. Marguerite Kohn, an orthodox Jewish refugee from Lyon, came to the plateau with her five children after her husband was arrested and deported. The family rented a home in the little hamlet of Flachet, and they were able to observe their faith openly while they lived there during the war. Their Protestant neighbors were understanding and helpful. Nobody complained when the Kohn children were absent from school on Saturdays—they understood that the Kohns were observing the Jewish Sabbath.

The Protestants' faith required them to help those in need. The pastors of the twelve villages on the plateau urged their followers to take in refugees. Without hesitation, the people of the plateau responded. All across La Montagne Protestante, Jewish refugees were quietly being sheltered.

Since 1938, the mayor of Le Chambon had been arranging shelter on the plateau for refugees who were fleeing Hitler's growing empire. Mayor Guillon warned the people of Le Chambon that they would soon need to house hundreds of refugee children, and that they should be prepared. In 1940, when France lost to the Nazis, Monsieur Guillon quit his job as mayor in protest against the Vichy government. He then spent the rest of the war working to care for refugees.

Right after the Nazis took over France, the two pastors of Le Chambon, André Trocmé and Edouard Theis, spoke out to their parishioners from the pulpit of their Protestant temple. Pastor Trocmé urged them to stand up against injustice in nonviolent ways, using "the weapons of the spirit."

In 1941, Pastor Trocmé offered his services to the Quakers, who were helping Jews imprisoned in the French internment camps. Pastor Trocmé was told that they didn't need his help in the camps, but that when the Quakers could get young people released, they didn't know where to send them. It was dangerous for anyone

Pastors Trocmé (right) and Theis of Le Chambon in their clerical clothing. They were outspoken against the Nazis and the Vichy government.

to take them in. Perhaps that was where he could help. Pastor Trocmé offered his village as a place of refuge.

When he returned to Le Chambon, his decision was put to a vote. It passed immediately. Le Chambon and the rest of La Montagne Protestante became the destination for many Jews, and especially Jewish children, released from the internment camps over the next four years.

Word spread that the plateau was a place that would welcome refugees. Sometimes fleeing refugees found their way to the home of a Protestant pastor, and the pastor or his wife would find a place for them. Sometimes, refugees simply showed up on people's doorsteps, asking for shelter. Jewish parents who were afraid of arrest sent their children to La Montagne Protestante. Oeuvre de Secours aux Enfants (OSE), a Jewish children's aid organization, found places for Jewish children on farms. Many times, children had to make the long journey without their parents. Nearly every day, a bus arrived or a train pulled into the station in Le Chambon carrying more children.

All these Jewish children needed somewhere to live. The area around Le Chambon already had a number of pensions. Pastor Trocmé approached the International Civil Service, a Swiss pacifist organization, to offer Le Chambon as a place for them to establish houses for children in need. Their motto was "Action, not words," and they were true to their motto. Their group, Swiss Aid for Children, set up three children's houses there, La Guespy, L'Abric, and Faïdoli, under the direction of a young Swiss man named August Bohny. Other organizations, such as the American

Quakers, the Salvation Army, and an international pacifist group called the Fellowship of Reconciliation, also helped, and by 1942, there were seven children's homes in Le Chambon funded by various charities.

Meantime, the inhabitants of La Montagne Protestante continued to open their arms to refugees. For example, the tiny hamlet of Les Tavas, a community of just ten farms, sheltered at least one Jewish child on every single farm. It is said that nearly every farm on the plateau sheltered a refugee.

Some people took in entire families, and sometimes Jewish refugee families rented farms or rooms in people's homes. Filmmaker Pierre Sauvage's parents, Jewish refugees, rented a room on a farm that belonged to the Roche family. Pierre was born there during the war. (Years later, Pierre came back to Le Chambon. He interviewed many people, and made *Weapons of the Spirit,* a compelling documentary film about what happened there during the war. He also created the Chambon Foundation, to keep the memory of the rescue effort alive.)

The Coblentz family, French Jewish refugees from the city of Strasbourg, came to the plateau and became farmers. The whole family pitched in on the farm. They named their pig Adolf, after Adolf Hitler!

Despite the refuge offered them by the inhabitants of La Montagne Protestante, Jewish children who had been released from the internment camps

Pierre Sauvage as a baby, being held by his father, in Le Chambon [Chambon Foundation]

Monsieur Coblentz and his son work on their farm on the plateau. [Chambon Foundation]

Adolf, the Coblentz family pig. He was named after Adolf Hitler. [Chambon Foundation]

and many of the other refugees were still in great danger. Children are always vulnerable during war, but Jewish children during World War II were actively hunted down and deported to death camps. The *gendarmes*—police—came repeatedly to Le Chambon looking for Jewish refugees in order to arrest them. These roundups were

Liberation, September 3, 1944, in Le Chambon. Pierre Bloch sits with two other boys and some French soldiers on their tank. He is fifth from the left. Pierre (who changed his name to Elyakim Ben-Gal when he moved to Israel as an adult) says of this photo: "My smile is both astonished and sad: astonished that the day we'd waited for so long had suddenly arrived, and sad because my best friend had died three weeks before."

frequent in the summer of 1942, when France began deporting Jews—including children and even babies—to the death camps in Poland.

Pierre Bloch and his family were French Jewish refugees from Lyon. They spent the summer of 1942 in a house in the center of Le Chambon that was owned by the Roussels, a Catholic family. They felt safe there, even when gendarmes came with buses to arrest Jews. Pierre recalls that Pastor Trocmé urged the people of the village not to cooperate with the gendarmes. Even though he was just a young boy, he remembers dozens of village women passing food through the bus window to the only person the gendarmes had managed to arrest.

No one can say now exactly who was responsible, but before most of the roundups in Le Chambon, people were warned and had time to take action. An emergency plan was in place: The young Jewish refugees would be taken by Boy Scouts to a safe hiding place. Some were hidden on farms—in the hayloft of a stable or in the middle of a woodpile. Every farm had a dog, and it would bark a warning whenever anyone approached. Sometimes, whole groups were sent to hide in the woods to pick blueberries or search for mushrooms all day—even when they weren't in season—until the gendarmes left and the all-clear signal was given. At times in the winter, the snow was so deep on the plateau that not even the gendarmes could get through.

Not all of the gendarmes were happy about what they had to do. Many of the people they were harrassing were their neighbors, and they had sympathy for the Jewish refugees. Sometimes the gendarmes would arrive in the village and go straight to the café, where they would spend half an hour eating and drinking and talking loudly about whom they had come to arrest. This was their way of giving a warning, allowing the café owner to spread the word. Then, later, when the gendarmes showed up to make the arrest, what a surprise! The person they were looking for was gone!

For some Jews, it was too risky to remain in France. They would receive false identification papers giving them a non-Jewish identity. Many people on the plateau

The Hôtel May in Le Chambon—many Jewish refugees lived here during the war. Gendarmes came to sit in the hotel's café when they wanted to give the Jews they were supposed to arrest some time to hide.

made these false papers. Oscar Rosowsky, a young Jewish refugee himself, recalls making false papers for fifty people a week, both for refugees and for the Resistance. It was very dangerous work. If anyone involved had been found out, he or she would certainly have been arrested.

After being given their new identity, the refugees were guided along a perilous route, two hundred miles to the border of Switzerland. They followed the same paths that had been taken by the Huguenots fleeing persecution centuries before.

At the border, refugees made the illegal crossing into Switzerland. They often had to sneak past armed guards patrolling with dogs, through barbed wire fences in the dead of night. Switzerland was a neutral country, which meant that it was not involved in the war. If the refugees were allowed to stay in Switzerland, they would be safe there. If not, they could be turned over to the French authorities and sent to an internment camp or deported.

Despite the danger, life for the refugee children on La Montagne Protestante was not all bad. Many of those who lived in group homes made close friends with their housemates, and those living on farms often developed strong attachments to the families that sheltered them.

Young refugees were able to attend school. Many didn't speak French, and so they had special French lessons. Generally, they learned pretty quickly.

The younger children attended the local elementary schools. Many of the older ones took classes at the Ecole Nouvelle Cévenole, a private, nontraditional, Protestant middle school and high school in Le Chambon. It was an exceptional place, and kids came from all over to go to school there. Some of the local boys and girls were enrolled as well. The Ecole Nouvelle Cévenole had been created in 1938 by Pastors Trocmé and Theis to promote peace and international unity. Contrary to French tradition, boys and girls were in classes together, no grades were given, and the school operated on an honor system. There was no other school like it in all of France.

During the war, teachers at the Ecole Nouvelle Cévenole were Protestants, agnostics, Catholics, and Jews. Some were refugees themselves. Many of them had been banned from teaching at the public schools in France. The quality of education was high. Although there was no library, the teachers loaned their own books to the students.

The school was not housed in one single building. Classes were held all over the place: in pensions, in unheated attics, in an unfinished house, in the basement of a pharmacy. Pastor Trocmé's wife, Magda, who was from Italy, taught Italian. One winter, her Italian class was held in the bathroom of a pension! Leather shoes were hard to find, so most people in Le Chambon wore *sabots*—wooden clogs—during the war. Students and teachers would leave their noisy sabots outside the classroom and wear slippers during class.

The Scouts were popular in France. In Le Chambon, there were Boy Scout troops and Girl Scout troops, and many refugees joined. The troops were made up of smaller groups, each of which had an animal totem. There were Foxes, Lions, Deer, Kangaroos, Squirrels, Grizzly Bears, and others. Sometimes kids only knew each other by their totem name.

Food was more plentiful on the plateau than in the cities, but there was often not enough. It was a constant struggle to gather enough food for all the refugees. Children's homes run by Swiss Aid for Children were lucky to receive extra supplies from Switzerland. Sometimes they got jam, halvah, cheese, and even chocolate.

Although many of the young refugees stayed busy with school, homework, Scouts, and friends, the war was never far away. Most of them had been separated from their families. Often, they did not know the fate of their relatives, or if they would ever see them again.

As the war progressed, things became worse. The Nazis took over France's Southern Zone in November 1942. Regional German army headquarters were set up in the nearby city of Le Puy-en-Velay. On the main street, in the middle of Le Chambon, German soldiers who were recuperating from war wounds filled the entire Hôtel du Lignon. The hotel was right next door to Tante Soly, a pension of Jewish children. Just up the hill was the home of Léon Eyraud, the head of the local French Resistance.

Since 1940, the people of La Montagne Protestante had maintained their independence and a spirit of defiance toward the Vichy government. They refused to accept the rule of an intolerant, hate-mongering government. They refused to ring the church bells in Maréchal (Marshal) Pétain's honor. At the Ecole Nouvelle Cévenole, they refused to hang his picture on the walls, to pledge an oath of allegiance, or even to salute the flag.

When a Vichy official named Lamirand came to Le Chambon to give a speech, very few people attended, and those that did, did not applaud. Afterward, a group of students from the Ecole Nouvelle Cévenole approached him with a letter they had written with Pastor Trocmé, and urged him to read it. The letter protested the mass arrests of Jews taking place in Paris. They wrote that there were Jews in Le Chambon, but that the people of Le Chambon saw no difference between Jews and non-Jews. They insisted that they would shelter Jews any time that they were in danger.

There is a motto carved in stone over the door of the Protestant temple in Le Chambon. It reads: *Aimez-vous les uns les autres,* which means "Love one another."

With the Germans in their midst, the people of La Montagne Protestante maintained their spirit. They continued to take in and shelter Jewish refugees at the risk of their own lives. They each followed their conscience, and weren't afraid to do what they knew was right.

The people of La Montagne Protestante lived by the words inscribed here, over the door to the Protestant temple in Le Chambon: *Aimez-vous les uns les autres*—"Love one another."

Elisabeth gathers blueberries in Le Chambon.

CHAPTER FOUR

Lost
Elisabeth

ELISABETH WAS BORN IN VIENNA, *Austria, on March 7, 1924. She was fourteen years old when the Nazis took over Austria. She arrived in Le Chambon when she was seventeen, and was twenty-one when the Allies achieved victory in Europe in 1945. She told us her story at her home in Alexandria, Virginia, when we interviewed her on October 3, 2002.*

Age 9—1933, Berlin, Germany

I saw the Nazis marching for the first time yesterday, and I felt so scared. I don't even know why. Vati [Dad] and Mutti [Mom] haven't said anything, but I know something is wrong. I can feel it.

Age 12—1936, Vienna, Austria

We left Berlin in such a hurry. We've moved back to Vienna, but instead of the nice big apartment that we lived in when I was little, we're living with Grandma and Grandpa. Vati doesn't have a job now.

My brother Peter and I are at school. In a couple of years, Peter will be going to university. He's four years older than me. I'm only twelve. I wish I could still go to Czisek Art School, like I did when we lived here before.

Age 14—March 1938, Vienna, Austria

The Nazis have taken over Austria! Vati has been working in Prague, and he wants us to join him there, but the Nazis won't let us leave the country because we're Jewish. And Vati can't come back, either.

His letters are frantic, telling us we have to get out of Austria. Mutti is trying everything, but she hasn't been able to get us visas to go anywhere, even though we already have passports.

VATI IS IN PARIS. Prague became too dangerous for Jews, and he finally got a visa to go to France. Mutti, Peter, and I still don't have visas, but we intend to join him there. We're going to try to escape from Austria, somehow.

Age 14—September 1938, Baden-Baden, Germany

We almost made it. We got on a tour bus that was going to France, but we were foolish. We brought a suitcase with us, and it made the police at the border suspicious. We were only supposed to be going for the day.

They stamped our passports to show that we had tried to enter France illegally, and they sent us back. Now anyone who looks at our passports will know, and it will be harder to escape.

Age 14—October 1938, Saarbrucken, Germany

We have boarded a train for France. I hope we get there this time. An SS officer on the train platform almost arrested us. Mutti pleaded with him to let us go. He did, but he smiled a nasty smile and said we'd never make it. He said if we got sent back again, we'd go straight to Dachau. We've heard whisperings about Dachau. They say it is some kind of prison camp. I'm terrified.

Age 14—November 1938, Cologne, Germany

The French police arrested us and put us in prison. Then they sent us back to Saarbrucken. When we got there, the same SS officer saw us. He didn't say anything, but he smiled his nasty smile again. After that, it was horrible. Some SS men put me in a room, and they took off all of my clothes. I was so scared. They beat me, then they finally left me alone.

Later, they let us all go. They had beaten Mutti and Peter, too.

Mutti managed to get in touch with Vati in Paris, and he told her to go to the French consulate here in Cologne. He's going to try to arrange for our visas.

MUTTI JUST GOT BACK from the French consulate. There were no visas for us. I think she's been crying. All of us are filthy and hungry and tired. We've been wearing the same clothes for days. Mutti seems to have lost all hope now. I've never seen her like this before.

Age 14—November 1938, Paris, France

Someone from the French consulate in Cologne saw my mother sitting on a park bench. She was trying to think of what to do next. He recognized her from the consulate and asked her if she had any jewelry. He took all of her jewelry in exchange for three visas, and we got on the next plane out of Germany. We were lucky! Vati met us at the airport and now we are all safe in Paris!

Age 15—April 1939, Paris, France

My old Latin teacher from Vienna, Fräulein Hoefert, came to live with us. She's Catholic, but she hates the Nazis, and didn't want to stay in Austria. But now she's leaving Paris, because she's found a job teaching in a village called Le Chambon.

I love living in Paris. It's such a beautiful city. My French is very good now. I'm even making a little money helping a neighbor with his correspondence. His French is terrible, and so is his German. He has a dreadful accent no matter what language he speaks! I also help Vati with his work. He writes a newsletter.

When we first got to Paris, we were so poor that we were hungry a lot. But then Vati started his newsletter. Now we have enough money to pay for a small apartment, and we have enough to eat.

I met someone I really like. His name is Ernest and he's a student from Czechoslovakia. He's seven years older than me—he's already twenty-two. We met in a bookstore. I introduced him to my parents right away, and they like him, too. He comes over often and talks politics with Vati.

Age 15—September 1939, Paris, France

Vati and Peter were taken to an internment camp. The Nazis have begun a war by invading Poland. Germany is now the enemy of France, and Austria is, too. Since we're Austrian, the French government considers us enemies, even though Nazi Germany hates us because we are Jews!

Age 15—March 1, 1940, Paris, France

I was a little nervous about starting art school in the middle of the year, but everyone's been so nice. The school wouldn't let me enroll at the beginning of the year because they said I was an enemy alien. But I finally convinced them to let me in, and now I'm in my second week of classes. I love it! All I've ever wanted to do is be an artist.

Age 16—March 7, 1940, Paris, France

This is the first time I've ever been alone on my birthday. I feel so sad and lonely. I had to make my own birthday dinner. I'm sixteen today.

I got some letters, and Peter sent me a poem. He and Vati are still in an internment camp, and Mutti is working as a nurse for a woman who lives in the suburbs. Ernest has been gone since he joined the Czech Army to fight the Nazis. I'm really worried about him.

Age 16—March 9, 1940, Paris, France

Today I got myself a bicycle. Now I can go places without having to pay for the train. I'm naming my bicycle Barthalomus.

Age 16—March 14, 1940, Paris, France

Vati came home today! The French government decided he wasn't an enemy after all. We didn't even know he had been released—he just showed up. But they won't let Peter out, and we can't even visit him. We tried to get permission. It was denied. What harm do they think it would possibly do if we visited him?

Age 16—April 1940, Paris, France

Ernest was here on leave. We spent eight whole days together! It was wonderful! We went for long walks and talked about our future. It was very romantic.

Vati and Mutti took us to the the-ater to celebrate my birthday, belatedly. I'm glad they like Ernest, too.

Age 16—May 1, 1940, Paris, France

I just got back from visiting Peter. We finally got permission, and I went to see him first. I took my bicycle, Barthalo-

Elisabeth made this small painting of herself and her boyfriend, Ernest, in her sketchbook in 1940.

mus, with me and rode back and forth from my hotel to the camp, three kilo-meters away. I spent a week there. He didn't know I was coming, and we were both so happy.

When I got home today, Vati was packing his bag. He's leaving again. He has to report as a *prestataire*—the government is making all foreigners work for the French Army.

Age 16—May 1940, Paris, France

Mutti and I are very worried. The Nazis have invaded Holland [the Nether-lands] and Belgium. France will be next. Foreign refugees like us are no longer safe. The government has been arresting anyone from Germany and the sur-rounding area and sending them to internment camps. They're even arresting women and children. Some of our neighbors have been taken away. Will they come for us?

Age 16—June 1, 1940, Paris, France

I just got some awful news! Ernest has written that he is being sent to the front lines. I wonder when I will ever see him again.

Age 16—June 11, 1940, Paris, France

The German army is in Paris. For days now, we've heard cannon fire and bombing. I spent a little time this afternoon walking around the Latin Quarter, saying good-bye to my favorite places. Mutti and I have packed a few things in two small sacks. I'm going to tie them onto the back of Barthalomus. Mutti and I are leaving.

Age 16—June 12, 1940, en route to St. Rémy, France

We had to sneak past the concierge this morning. She had said she would turn us in if we tried to leave. Everyone is fleeing Paris. We're heading south, along with everybody else. I asked and asked and finally found some people who would take Mutti in their car. We'll go wherever they're heading, as long as it's south. They're going to St. Rémy. Mutti and I will meet there. I'll go by bicycle.

Age 16—June 12, 1940, St. Rémy, France

Mutti and I forgot to arrange a place to meet in St. Rémy, and it's very crowded here. There are so many people, I don't know how I'm going to find her. It's raining and I've been waiting here for hours, sitting with my bicycle at the edge of town. I'm tired and hungry and soaking wet, but I'm afraid to leave, in case I miss her.

Age 16—June 13, 1940, en route to Chartres, France

Mutti didn't arrive in St. Rémy until very late, because the road had been clogged with cars. So many people were looking for a place to stay, and the hotels were already full. Some people were even lying down to sleep on the wet streets. Luckily, a nice Polish woman offered to let us stay in her apartment.

We've decided that from now on, wherever we go, we'll meet at the town hall.

Age 16—June 13, 1940, Chartres, France

The Germans are bombing Chartres. I got here and found Mutti, and now they're telling us to go into the bomb shelter. I haven't eaten all day. Earlier, I had an anxiety attack. I was trembling and crying, and I felt so ashamed. That was before I found Mutti.

Age 16—June 14, 1940, Chartres, France

I can't sleep. This bench is so hard and I'm so angry. Mutti and I were arrested. They think we're German spies! The police looked through my bag and found my book of German poetry, my diary, my sketchbook, and Ernest's passport and identity papers. This is so stupid! If I really were a spy, I wouldn't have had those things with me.

The police questioned us for hours, and all they gave us to eat was a hardboiled egg. Finally, they turned out the light and told us we had to sleep here. When we asked if they would let us go in the morning, they wouldn't answer. Even though I'm exhausted, I'm too frustrated and angry to fall asleep on this hard wooden bench.

Elisabeth's painting of herself and her mother being arrested by gendarmes

It's five o' clock in the morning. Someone opens the door. "Run, run, the Germans are coming," he shouts. I grab Mutti's hand, and we go.

Age 16—June 1940, outskirts of Blois, France

I've lost Mutti. We were supposed to meet in Vendôme, but she never came. Then I went to the internment camp near Blois, where Vati was supposed to be, but everyone was gone. Finally, I collapsed under a tree. When I woke up, I was surrounded by four Belgian soldiers. They gave me some sugar to eat, and they told me I couldn't stay there, that the Germans were coming.

The soldiers came with me to Blois. I hoped Mutti might be there, also looking for Vati. When we got here, the French Army wouldn't let us cross the bridge into town because they were about to blow it up. I tried to rush across anyway, but they stopped me.

I ran off by myself and cried and cried.

Age 16—June 1940, Toulouse, France

The Belgian soldiers have been so nice to me. They traveled with me all the way here to Toulouse. We ate whatever food we could find in the fields, and we slept where we could. I asked everyone we met if they had seen any of my family. I met someone who said he had seen my brother in Toulouse, so now I am here. But there are so many refugees, I don't know how I can possibly find him.

I looked everywhere for Peter. No one I asked had seen him. I was ready to give up. And then, by some miracle I saw him! He was standing at the end of the street selling newspapers. I couldn't believe it was him! I've found my brother!

PETER IS LATE. We were supposed to meet here at the post office at ten o'clock. I'm tired of standing and waiting, so I wander over to the counter. On impulse, I ask if there's a letter for me. And the clerk hands me a letter! Who could it be from? No one even knows I'm in Toulouse.

It's from Mutti! She says she's working as a nurse in Pau, and she's sending letters addressed to me to ten different cities in France, in the hope that one of them will reach me. One of them has! I've found Mutti!

Age 17—June 1941, Saint Sauveur par Bellac, France

I can hardly believe it, but I've found my entire family, even Ernest! Peter is living in Toulouse with his girlfriend, and Ernest is studying in Grenoble. Mutti, Vati, and I are living in Saint Sauveur par Bellac, but Vati says it's not safe here.

We got a letter from Fräulein Hoefert, my old Latin teacher. She says I should come to Le Chambon, where she is teaching. I can work as an *au pair*, taking care of the children of the village's pastor, Pastor Trocmé. She says it would be much safer for me there, and Vati says I have to go.

Age 17—July 1941, Le Chambon-sur-Lignon, France

I never realized how rambunctious and energetic little children could be. I'm so exhausted at the end of the day after taking care of the Trocmé children. Nelly is different. She's fourteen, three years younger than me, and very independent. I don't have to take care of her. We've become friends. She plays the piano beautifully. It's the three boys, always fighting and full of mischief, that I take care of from morning to night.

I also help with household chores. The Trocmés have several boarders, and there's so much work to do. Mama Trocmé is always taking care of everybody. Meanwhile, Pastor Trocmé is busy with his work, so the children rarely get to spend time with him. They constantly crave his attention.

There's only one time each day when this busy household quiets down. That's when Pastor Trocmé comes out of his study for dinner, and everyone sits at the table together. He says a prayer, and then we all sing the same song every evening. It is very simple, and very beautiful. The first time I heard it, I nearly cried.

You who have
All things
And give them to us each day.
Receive, O Father,
Our prayer
Of gratitude and love.

Age 17—September 1941, Le Chambon-sur-Lignon, France

Pastor Trocmé has asked me to help the refugee children who are coming to Le Chambon. It means I will have to leave the Trocmés. He wants me to live in a children's home called La Guespy. Many of the children who will be there won't understand French, only German. They've been living in an internment camp called Gurs, and they're coming here alone, without their parents. The pastor says that I can help them to adjust.

I've started to love the Trocmés and I don't want to leave, but I will do what Pastor Trocmé thinks is best.

Age 17—September 1941, Le Chambon-sur-Lignon, France

These children are so desperately unhappy and scared. They cry at night, and they have terrible nightmares. All I can do is sit with them and hold their hands. They need someone to listen to them and comfort them. I'm doing all I can.[45]

EVERY DAY WE GATHER CHESTNUTS and blueberries, when we can find them. There's not really enough food for growing children at La Guespy, especially teenage boys. Some of them are always hungry. One boy got in trouble for stealing a potato. I felt sorry for him. He didn't mean to be bad, his body just needed more food.

Mademoiselle Usach is in charge of the house. We try not to have anything to do with each other. She's much too strict. I've become close friends with Hanne (see chapter 26, "Love in Wartime: Hanne and Max"). She came here from Gurs and is my age.

Age 17—November 1941, Le Chambon-sur-Lignon, France

I got a letter from Vati. We have visas for America! He says I have to leave Le Chambon immediately and meet them in Lyon.

The children need me here at La Gue-

Elisabeth, wearing skis, dances around a snowman with Lilli, a Jewish refugee who was sent to La Guespy from the Gurs internment camp.

spy. It's so hard to think of leaving, but I miss my family, too. Anyway, Vati is expecting me, so I'll leave for Lyon tomorrow.

IT'S SNOWING HARD, and I'm lost. I waited for the train in Le Chambon. It never came. It's seventy-five kilometers to Lyon, but I decided to walk. Then I fell and got stuck in the snow. I was sure that I was going to freeze to death. Somehow I got up and started to run. But the snow is up to my knees and I'm so cold.

I can't see where the road is. I can't go forward, but I can't turn back. I'm lost.

EPILOGUE

Elisabeth Kaufmann Koenig did make it to Lyon, although the experience was so traumatic that she had no memory of the journey after being lost in the snow. From Lyon, her family eventually crossed the border into Spain on December 7, 1941, just before the border between Spain and France was closed.

In February 1942, they sailed out of Lisbon for America. Their ship stopped first in Cuba, where her grandparents had settled, but they were not allowed off the ship to find them. Then the ship stopped in the Bahamas, where the police came on board and arrested several passengers as German spies.

The Kaufmanns finally disembarked at the military base in Virginia Beach. From there, they were guided blindfolded through the base to a train with blacked-out windows, which took them to New York, their final destination.

Elisabeth arrived in New York knowing only two words of English, "to" and "cheek," which she learned from the song "Cheek to Cheek." She attended a year of high school, taking extra classes to learn English, and then went on to Hunter College.

Her brother, Peter, got married. He and his wife were expecting a baby when he enlisted in the U.S. Army. In 1944, Peter died fighting the Nazis in France, at the age of twenty-four.

After the war, Elisabeth learned that Ernest had survived, despite three years in Auschwitz, and was living in England.

They married in 1947, settled in the United States, and have one daughter and one granddaughter.

Elisabeth continued to paint and also worked as a librarian for many years, eventually creating the library at the U.S. Holocaust Memorial Museum in Washington, D.C.

Ernest worked for the American Foreign Service, and they lived all over the world, including Paris and Bonn, Germany.

Elisabeth said that she didn't bear hatred toward anyone for what happened during the war, and that she and Ernest didn't want their daughter to learn hatred, either.

The experience of living with the Trocmés in Le Chambon affected Elisabeth deeply. She said that "Mama Trocmé was a wonderful, caring person who did everything" and that "in the few months that I had lived in their house I had learned moral principles that shaped my life."

Elisabeth passed away in April 2003.

The Protestant temple in Le Chambon in wintertime [Chambon Foundation]

CHAPTER FIVE

Guiding Spirits
The Pastors

Dᴜʀɪɴɢ ᴛʜᴇ ᴡᴀʀ, the pastors of the thirteen parishes of La Montagne Protestante worked to find shelter among their parishioners for the refugees flowing onto the plateau. All the pastors also opened their own homes to refugees.

Each pastor had his own network. The pastors met from time to time to keep in touch, and some of them passed on information at Bible study groups and Sunday services. They had passwords for messengers and guides to use, which were changed monthly. They had special codes which they used to communicate with one another. For instance, the name "Hans" was a code word for "German." These codes were especially necessary for letters that might be intercepted or for telephone conversations that might be overheard by outsiders.

In code, Jewish refugees were sometimes referred to as "Old Testaments." This was a reference to the fact that the Jewish Bible consists of the Old Testament of the Christian faith. A pastor might receive a note from another, saying, "I am sending you two 'Old Testaments.'" Then he would find shelter for the two Jewish refugees among his parishioners.

André Bettex, a pastor in Le Mazet, organized a group of Boy Scouts to help him in this work. One day in 1942, one of the Scouts came to his house to tell him about a group of young Jewish refugees from Germany and Austria who needed places to hide. Pastor Bettex immediately went to find farmers willing to take them in. Then, he and the Scouts brought the refugees to those farms.

After a while, however, it became too dangerous for them to stay. Pastor Bettex, with the help of a student who lived in nearby Freycenet, found the refugees Scout uniforms to wear as a disguise and guided them on foot toward Switzerland. They taught them a Swiss song, "High Up on the Mountain," and they all sang as they walked through the villages of the plateau. The *gendarmes*—police—who had been looking for the young refugees several days earlier, opened their windows to watch the "Boy Scouts" as they passed by, singing in the pouring rain!

The pastor of Freycenet, Charles Delizy, had once been a radio technician in the army. During the Occupation, he worked with the Resistance, receiving coded radio messages and passing them along. He took a great risk by keeping the radio transmitter in his own home.

Daniel Curtet, pastor of Fay-sur-Lignon, arranged for refugees to illegally receive food rationing cards. False authorization cards were parachuted in from England. They were hidden by Pastor Poivre, a retired pastor in Le Chambon, in books in his library, until Pastor Curtet could take them to the town hall in Les Vastres and exchange them for authentic ration cards. This exchange was dangerous, but the secretary of the town hall told him not to worry. His boss was on their side.

Daniel Besson was pastor of one of the smallest parishes on the plateau, in Montbuzat. It was made up of 135 families, whose farms and homes were spread in a three-and-a-half-mile circle around their temple. There was no hotel, no *pension—*

The two children of Pastor Marc Donadille hold hands with a tiny Jewish refugee (center). Pastor Donadille was part of CIMADE, a French Protestant rescue organization, during the war. Donadille and his brother, who worked for the French railroad, helped many Jewish refugees reach the safety of La Montagne Protestante, and then go on to Switzerland.

boardinghouse—not even any rooms to rent. The only places for refugees were with the 135 families of the parish.

The ideal place to hide refugees was in an isolated house, preferably in a room that had more than one door, in case a quick escape became necessary. It was also best if the family didn't have young children, who might not understand the need to be discreet about their houseguests. However, many families did have young children. They would be taught never to mention the strangers staying in their home to anyone. In the morning before school, each mother would put a finger to her lips and say, "Shhh," as a reminder.

To make sure that everybody was safe—the refugees and the families that hid them—Pastor Besson had two rules. The refugees had to hide whenever anyone approached, even neighbors or relatives; and the only time they could come out was in the dead of night. The system worked very well.

Pastor André Trocmé and his wife, Magda, worked throughout the war to help refugees. [Chambon Foundation]

Pastor André Morel was a skilled mountain climber. He guided refugees across the mountains into Switzerland for an organization called CIMADE (Comité Inter-Mouvements Auprès Des Evacués). He was caught and put in prison. When he was released in 1942, he was sent to La Montagne Protestante to be the pastor of Devesset. There, he continued to aid refugees. He also joined the Resistance and helped them to get supplies to the *maquis*—Resistance fighters.

Pastors André Trocmé and Edouard Theis of Le Chambon were committed pacifists. Pacifists believe in finding nonviolent solutions to all disputes. Pastors Trocmé and Theis believed in only nonviolent resistance to the Nazis. They were active pacifists, and were not afraid to speak out against injustice.

Le Chambon was known to the Nazis and to the Vichy government as a haven for Jewish refugees. One day in 1942, the gendarmes arrived in Le Chambon with buses. They intended to arrest all the Jews there, fill the buses with them, and take them away. When Pastor Trocmé was asked for a list identifying all the Jewish refugees in Le Chambon, he refused, saying, "I don't know the names of the Jews here, and even if I had such a list, I wouldn't give it to you. They came here to the Protestants on the plateau seeking refuge and protection. I am their pastor, their shepherd, and it is not the role of the shepherd to denounce the sheep that have been placed in his care." Their response to him was blunt: If Trocmé refused to help, it would be *he* who would be arrested and deported instead. He still refused.

In February 1943, Pastor Trocmé was arrested along with Pastor Theis and Roger Darcissac, the head of the public school in Le Chambon. Monsieur Darcissac not only protected the Jewish refugee children who attended his school, but he also helped the refugees in many other ways. The three men were seen by some as the driving force behind the rescue effort. They were sent to an internment camp. After four weeks they were released, but several months later, the two pastors had to go into hiding. It was being rumored that they would be arrested again, or possibly assassinated.

Pastor Trocmé remained in hiding for nearly a year. During that period, Pastor Theis worked with CIMADE, guiding Jewish refugees to Switzerland, until he was arrested for helping them cross the border illegally. Both pastors came back to Le Chambon right before the liberation of the plateau.

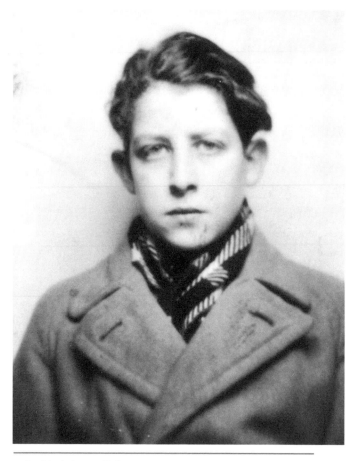

Rudi in Antwerp, Belgium, 1940

CHAPTER SIX

Lighting Hanukkah Candles
Rudi

RUDI WAS BORN IN MANNHEIM, *Germany, on May 13, 1925. He was thirteen years old on Kristallnacht—the Night of Broken Glass—and fourteen when the Nazis invaded Poland and World War II began. He came to Le Chambon at the age of seventeen. When the Allies achieved victory in Europe in 1945, he was nearly twenty years old. He told us his story in New York City when we interviewed him on October 24, 2002.*

Age 12—1937, Mannheim, Germany

I've decided to change my name. I don't like the name Rudolf, or even Rudi. I'd rather have a sophisticated American name, like Denny. I read that it's very popular there. I told everyone in my family to call me Denny from now on, but they keep forgetting and calling me Rudi.

This Jewish-owned business in Berlin, Germany, was one of the many Jewish properties targeted on *Kristallnacht*—the Night of Broken Glass.

Age 13—Kristallnacht, November 10, 1938, Mannheim, Germany

Early this morning the Gestapo—Nazi secret police—arrested Papa and took him away. After that, a mob gathered in front of our building. Ten Nazis broke down our door and used their axes to destroy everything in our apartment, the furniture, everything. They stole Mama's jewelry, and now they're throwing hundreds of books from Papa's library out the windows. They didn't even bother to open the windows, and now all the glass is broken. I can see down to the street below. They're setting fire to piles of books. They're burning all the books! Not just ours—the piles are huge.

It's a good thing my older brother, Martin, isn't home. The Nazis might have beaten him up or even arrested him. I don't think they'll arrest me because I'm only thirteen. They haven't hurt me or Mama, but our apartment is in ruins.

Mama says thank goodness Martin is leaving the country soon. He has a visa to go to the United States. Mama says it's hard to get visas to go anywhere, but we all have to leave Germany somehow. My family has lived in Germany for hundreds of years. But Mama says we have to go.

THINGS ARE SO DIFFERENT NOW. We used to live in a big house, and when I was little I had a nanny and lots of toys. Papa was an attorney and a judge. He had important jobs. I had always been first or second in my class. Latin was my favorite subject, and I think the teachers really liked me. But then things started to change. Kids beat me up at school just because I was Jewish. The other Jewish kid in my class got beaten up, too. Some kids defended us, but it was really tough.

Then the government passed all these new laws. First, Jews couldn't work for the government anymore, so Papa lost his job as a judge. Later, they said Jews couldn't own houses anymore, either. So we moved to this little apartment. And now the apartment is ruined. And they've taken Papa to the Dachau concentration camp.

Age 13—March 1939, Driebergen, the Netherlands

I miss Mama so much. The last thing she did before I left home was show me how to sew on a button. She said I'm going to be alone for a while, and I'll have to take care of myself.

Martin is in America now, and Papa is, too. They're living in Philadelphia, where we have relatives. We can't get permanent visas for the United States right now, but Mama found out that the American consulate was giving out some visitors' visas. She went all the way to Stuttgart to get one for Papa. Once he had a visa, they released him from Dachau. He left for America five days later. All he was allowed to take was a suitcase of clothing. Nothing else, not even money.

Mama and I couldn't get visas. She paid a *passeur*—a people smuggler—a lot of money to sneak me over the border to Holland [the Netherlands]. The passeur picked me up in Cologne. All I brought was a knapsack with some extra clothes in it.

The passeur drove a whole group of us in an old car to a farmhouse, where we waited for a while. Late that night, he led us through fields and forests for hours. Then he stopped and said, "You are now in Holland, you are now safe!"

He must have paid off the border guards, because we didn't see any. I didn't know exactly where the borderline was, but, suddenly, there we were—we had crossed into Holland.

Somebody from a Jewish refugee committee was waiting for us. He took me to a children's home in Wijk aan Zee. After that, they moved me to a shelter for refugees in Driebergen. We've started classes here, and I'm learning Dutch.

Age 14–15—1940, Rotterdam, the Netherlands

I'm at a real school now, a good school. It's called the Erasmiaans Gymnasium. My teachers are really nice to me. My Dutch is a little better, but I have to learn French and Latin in Dutch, and that's hard when German is your native language! I have to translate everything into German first, in my head. But I like it here a lot because everybody treats me as an equal. I think they respect me.

The Jewish *weeshuis*—orphanage—where I'm living is great, too. It's on a tree-lined street, and most of the children are Dutch. There are a lot of rules, but I like it because it's organized. The last place I lived, the Achterklooster, in the center of town, was not so nice. It was huge and nobody paid much attention to us kids.

Mama writes me at least twice a week from Belgium. A passeur brought her there a few months ago. She couldn't find one to bring her to Holland. In her letters, she gives me lots of advice: "Make sure that you are always clean. Make sure you take a bath every week. Do your homework, be polite to the elders, help younger children, say your prayers every night, go to synagogue on Fri-

Rudi on his way to school in Rotterdam, Holland, 1940

day night." She includes a *coupon réponse*—a coupon for a stamp—in each letter so that I don't have to pay for a stamp to write her back.

I do go to synagogue every week, with other children from the weeshuis. Afterward, families invite us back to their homes for Sabbath dinner. For a few hours I am part of someone's family.

Age 15—May 14, 1940, Rotterdam, the Netherlands

The city is in flames! The Germans invaded Holland four days ago. This morning we all had to run down into the basement when the bombs began to fall. We were down there for hours, and we could hear all the explosions. Any second, a bomb could have hit our building.

Finally the bombing stopped and we came upstairs. Everyone is saying that lots of German soldiers have parachuted in and they've taken over the city—or what's left of it.

I can't believe our building is still standing. All around us, buildings have been flattened. Lots of people must have died. Everything's on fire, and there's smoke everywhere.

Mr. onderwijzer, the director of the weeshuis, says we can go in now. Our building is safe, but I hate that the Nazis are here in Holland.

Age 15—October 1940, Rotterdam, the Netherlands

When I came home from school today, Mr. Onderwijzer told me, "You're leaving for Belgium tomorrow." I'm going to live with Mama! I can't wait! It's been two years since I've seen her, and I haven't even heard from her in months.

Now that the Nazis control both Holland and Belgium, there's less of a problem crossing the border, so I can join Mama. I leave for Antwerp in the morning!

Age 16—December 1941, Brussels, Belgium

Papa has been trying everything to get us visas to come to America. Nothing is working. He says our only chance now is to go to France. The American consulate there might give us visas, but we have to go to Marseille to get them. I'm not in school anymore, even though I'm only sixteen. The school here wouldn't let me in. I think it's because my French isn't good enough—all the classes are taught in French.

Mama says we can scrape together enough money to pay a passeur to take us into France. We'll need another passeur to cross the border between Nazi-occupied France and southern France. Marseille is on the southern coast.

Age 16–17—1942, Rivesaltes internment camp, France

We never made it to Marseille. We got arrested by *gendarmes*—policemen—as soon as we crossed into southern France. They brought us here, to an internment camp called Rivesaltes. Mama is in the women's barracks and I'm in the men's barracks. But we can see each other through the fence.

So many people are dying here. When they get sick, there's no medicine. There's not enough to eat. The cooks in the kitchen are the most popular people in the camp. It's better to be a cook than to be a king! The cooks give extra food to whomever they want, and they sell it illegally, too.

Dr. Neter is being held here, too. We know him from Mannheim. He's in charge of the hospital barrack and thanks to him, Mama can work there with him. The camp needs them.

Papa got us visas to Cuba, but then the Cuban consulate left Mama's name off the letter they sent here. The commandant of Rivesaltes says I should go to Marseille to get my visa. Mama can't come with me. Maybe there's a visa for her, but since her name wasn't in the letter, she can't go. I'm going to have to stay at Les Milles until my visa comes through. Les Milles is another internment camp near Marseille.

Age 17—August 1942, Les Milles internment camp, France

Since I got here, they've started deporting people and sending them away in cattle cars. The rumors are that they're being sent to work in Nazi factories, but no one is sure. Everyone says that if they want us to work then they'll have to feed us. That might be true, but I'm afraid of being sent back to Germany, all the same. I don't know what to believe.

I've heard they're deporting people from all the camps in France. I hope Mama will be safe. They need workers in the hospital barrack so maybe they won't put her on the deportation list yet.

Every few days, a big group of us gets deported. First they make us stand on one side of the courtyard, all together in a group. They read off names from their list, alphabetically. If you hear your name called, you have to go stand in a group on the other side of the courtyard. If you don't hear your name called, you're supposed to stay right where you are. Sometimes they deport one group, and sometimes they deport the other. We don't know until the last moment who is getting deported and who is staying. So far, I'm still here.

Age 17—September 1942, Les Milles internment camp, France

They haven't called my name, Appel. They're still calling the A's, but I haven't heard my name yet. Now they're calling the B's. I guess they're not going to call my name. I wonder which group is going to be deported this time. I look around at the people who are left standing with me.

Suddenly, I don't know why, I start walking. I walk across the courtyard and join the other group, even though they never called my name. Now I'm waiting to find out what will happen to me.

THIS GROUP IS STAYING and the other group is being deported. I still don't know why I walked away from them, but if I hadn't, I'd be in a cattle car, too.

This is the courtyard at Les Milles where Rudi waited to learn his fate.

Age 17—September 1942, Rivesaltes internment camp, France

They've closed down Les Milles camp, so now I'm back in Rivesaltes. I didn't even have time to contact the Cuban consulate. I can forget about my visa.

It almost feels like coming home, because I know people here. Some of them are really nice, like Fräulein Reiter, from Swiss Aid for Children. The Quakers and the YMCA (Young Men's Christian Association) are also here trying to help us.

Mama is gone, though. The doctor who's been protecting her, Dr. Neter, made up a story that she was very sick, so the camp commandant sent her to a prison hospital in Perpignan. Dr. Neter did that to keep her from being deported. She's safe for now.

I'm safe now, too, because they just changed the rules—for the moment, they're not deporting anyone seventeen and under without a parent.

FRÄULEIN REITER JUST GAVE ME the most incredible news! I'm leaving the camp! She's arranged to get some of us out of Rivesaltes. Children who are alone here will be sent to live in Swiss Aid homes for refugees, and she wants me to go, too. I'm going to La Guespy, a group home in a village called Le Chambon.

Age 18—December 1943, Le Chambon-sur-Lignon, France

Tonight is the first night of Hanukkah, and I've organized a Hanukkah party. There are about twenty-five of us refugee kids living here. We're not all Jewish, but Mademoiselle Usach said we could have the party. I've even taught her how to play the Hanukkah song "Maoz Tsur" (Rock of Ages) on the piano. She's the director of La Guespy, and she's very strict, but we get along.

The party's going to be in the common room. It's the only room in the house that's warm because it's the only room with a stove. We'll light Hanukkah candles in there.

There's no synagogue in Le Chambon, but the pastor gave us a room in their temple. The Latin teacher at the school is a Jewish refugee, and he holds Friday night services there for us.

I really like it here. The food is good and we have enough of it. My bed is clean. Even the air is pure and wonderful up here in the mountains. I share a room with some other boys. All the boys are on the top floor, the girls are on the second floor, and we all share one bathroom!

I'm going to the Ecole Nouvelle Cévenole. It's a very good school, like the Erasmiaans Gymnasium in Holland. I go to school, I do my homework, we walk around, we flirt with the girls. Some kids are only here for a month or two. Mostly they're French kids here for their summer vacation. Some of us stay a lot longer.

There are other Swiss Aid homes in Le Chambon, and lots of refugees live here. There are even some German soldiers living in a hotel in town, but they mind their own business. I think they're wounded soldiers from the Russian front. They seem to be happy just being here, and they don't bother anybody.

Sometimes the Jewish refugee kids have to

La Guespy, 1944. The Swiss flag hangs from the balcony railing. Mademoiselle Usach is standing on the left. Rudi is on the right, peering over someone's shoulder. He slept in the upper left-room in this picture.

hide in the woods. There always seems to be a warning when there's going to be a *razzia*—a police raid. The villagers tell us not to sleep in our beds that night, and Mademoiselle Usach sends us into the woods with blankets to stay overnight. Then someone finds us when it's safe to come back. I'm not worried—I know the villagers are looking out for us.

I like it here. I know where I belong, I know this is my place. I don't know what will happen. I don't know how this war will end, but for now, Le Chambon is a good place to be.

Rudi bringing a cart full of provisions back to La Guespy. He is holding a round loaf of bread.

WE LIT THE HANUKKAH CANDLES and it was beautiful, but I couldn't help thinking about Mama. She's in hiding in the town of Grenoble, being hidden in a room in someone's house. She can't go outside at all or make any noise. No one even knows she's living in that back room. I worry about her all the time.

Age 19—September 1944, Le Chambon-sur-Lignon, France

It's over! The Germans are on the run! French soldiers came through Le Chambon today in tanks. I'm safe at last! When the soldiers reach Grenoble, Mama will be safe, too. Everyone in Le Chambon is celebrating!

The children of La Guespy dancing to celebrate the liberation of Le Chambon.

Epilogue

Rudi Appel and his mother lived in Grenoble for a year after the war finally ended in 1945. They were reunited with his father and brother in Philadelphia in 1946. He changed the spelling of his name to Rudy after he came to the United States.

Although Rudy wanted very much to go to college, he had no money to pay for it, and so he found work instead. He started his career as a furrier, then he became a salesman for an export company. He added Spanish to the other languages he had learned, and he has used them all in his work. He has traveled on business to eighty-two different countries. He continues to work, and has no plans to retire.

Rudy has been very involved in charity work. During the time that Russia was still part of the Soviet Union, he worked with an organization that helped many Soviet Jewish families imigrate to Israel and the United States to live. He is still very involved with a synagogue of former Soviet Jews in Brooklyn, New York.

He married a German Jewish woman, and they have two daughters and three grandchildren. He and his wife live in New York.

Rudy has been back to Le Chambon several times. Working for the Chambon Foundation, he has been involved in the establishment and development of a museum right in the center of the village that chronicles the rescue by the villagers of many Jewish children and adults during the Holocaust.

He says, "I have been asked repeatedly what it felt like to be alone, without my family, as a child in a foreign country. I think that there was an overwhelming feeling of powerlessness. Powerlessness is an awful feeling. I do not mean power over another person. I mean a feeling of not having control of one's own life. On the contrary, I was completely dependent on others. This feeling of powerlessness is not to be confused with being worthless. I knew I was worthy. My parents had done a good job of instilling it in me. I was a member of an old civilization. My ancestors had been present when the Ten Commandments were given. Western civilization rests on those Commandments."

A snowball fight at Faïdoli, one of the group homes run by Swiss Aid
for Children in Le Chambon [Chambon Foundation]

CHAPTER SEVEN

One Big Family
Swiss Aid for Children and August Bohny

AUGUST BOHNY TOLD US *about his experiences in Le Chambon during the war when we interviewed him at his home in Basel, Switzerland, on November 9, 2002.*

AUGUST BOHNY HAD ALWAYS WANTED to work with children. He came to France from Switzerland in 1941, when he was a very young man. Swiss Aid for Children was created by concerned Swiss citizens. In the middle of the war, it became part of the new Swiss Red Cross and was able to do even more to help children. Swiss Aid for Children sent Monsieur Bohny to Le Chambon to run children's homes there. Eventually, three children's homes around Le Chambon were established under his direction, with a staff to help. In addition, Monsieur Bohny came up with the idea for a farm school, where teenagers could live while learning all about farming, and

Teenagers learn to make a chair in the Atelier Cévenol—the woodworking workshop set up by August Bohny.

he set up a carpentry workshop to teach woodworking.

The children staying in the Swiss Aid homes were not all Jewish refugees. Some were orphans and some were war refugees from other countries. In fact, some of the children were not refugees at all—they were children from the cities of France, where there were deadly air raids and severe food shortages. These children were sent to a Swiss Aid home by their parents for a short time, to be safe, and to enjoy the benefits of life on the plateau. Officially, this was the purpose of the Swiss Aid homes—to give French children a respite from the hardships and danger of the war. Jewish children blended in with the rest, and no one talked about it. Altogether, by the end of the war, Monsieur Bohny's Swiss Aid homes had cared for about one thousand children.

Despite the fact that Switzerland sent extra supplies, Monsieur Bohny's biggest challenge was finding enough food for all the children. Even the extra food coupons given to teenagers still didn't provide them with enough food. In fact, everyone caring for refugees on La Montagne Protestante was constantly struggling with this problem. The farm school that Monsieur Bohny set up provided some food, but there were about seventy-five children living in all three Swiss Aid homes at any one time. Growing children and teenagers require a lot of food!

Shortly after Monsieur Bohny arrived, the local cows stopped giving milk. Nobody could figure out why. Monsieur Joseph was in charge of stocking the larder. For a time, he had to go every other day by train to the neighboring hamlet, and then walk from farm to farm, carrying large milk cans, to look for milk. He would gather a gallon here and a gallon there, and then lug the cans back to Le Chambon. When the snow was too deep, he wouldn't make it back with the milk until the following day.

Monsieur Bohny met often with Pastor Trocmé. They discussed ideas and problems, and the pastor helped him to find the things he needed for the children's homes. During the time when Pastors Trocmé and Theis were under arrest, Monsieur Bohny played the organ and led the choir at the Protestant temple. The members of the choir included many of the shopkeepers of the village. He got to know them, and they were very generous to the children's homes.

Children outgrow their clothing quickly, and many refugees arrived with nothing. Various organizations provided clothing for them. The children would pass clothing down to smaller housemates whenever they outgrew something. Shoes were a different matter. Not only were they outgrown, but they also wore out quickly. At times, there were children whose shoes were in such poor condition that they couldn't even go outside when the weather was bad. Monsieur Bohny got them *sabots*—wooden clogs—to wear if he couldn't find them other shoes.

Monsieur Bohny ruled his homes with love. The children called him Papa Gusti— Gusti was short for August, his first name. They adored him. For much of the war, he lived at L'Abric, where the youngest children were only five years old. He became a father to many of them. Every night, he kissed each one good night before turning out the light, and he spent extra time with those who were sad or homesick. He insisted that the directors of the other two Swiss Aid homes do the same.

Children from La Guespy, one of the Swiss Aid homes, perform a song they've prepared. Mademoiselle Usach, the director of La Guespy, stands at right. Joseph Atlas (see Chapter Twenty-five, "The Bad Boy of La Guespy: Joseph") is behind her to the left, and Pastor Trocmé is seated on the right.

The group spirit of the homes was very strong. Monsieur Bohny taught the children Swiss songs, and every night after dinner they would all sing together. He says, "The children knew more Swiss songs than Swiss children themselves!" Every Sunday the children from all the homes would get together and perform songs and skits for one another that they had prepared in secret. Sometimes Pastor Trocmé would come and tell them stories. He was a masterful storyteller, and the children loved listening to him.

There were times when the Jewish children had to hide from the *gendarmes*— police. Someone in the Swiss Aid homes kept watch, and any time there was going to be a raid, the Jewish children would be taken out into the woods to hide. They would stay there until they got the signal that it was safe to return. Often the gendarmes came in the middle of the night. The three children's homes were about a mile apart, so if someone in one home saw the gendarmes approaching, he or she would flick the lights on and off to signal the other homes. During the day, the warning signal was a big sheet hung across a window.

Not all of the children in the three Swiss Aid homes were young. La Guespy, which had already been established before Monsieur Bohny arrived in Le Chambon, was set up for teenage refugees from the French internment camps. The oldest refugees were eighteen years old, only a few years younger than Monsieur Bohny himself.

For ten days, in the summer of 1942, a dozen Jewish teenagers from La Guespy came each night to sleep at L'Abric. They were in danger of being arrested and felt safer under the same roof as Monsieur Bohny. He put mattresses out on the living room floor for them. Then, in the middle of one night, the gendarmes came to the door. They demanded that Monsieur Bohny hand over the Jewish kids. He refused, insisting that the children in his care were under Swiss protection. The gendarmes left to consult their superiors, telling him that they would be back in the morning, and that the children had better be there.

In the early morning, Monsieur Bohny awakened the youngsters, fed them breakfast, and had them sent to farms across the plateau to be hidden. When the gendarmes returned to arrest them all, they were gone. The gendarmes were so furious that they threatened to arrest Monsieur Bohny instead.

The farmers took seriously their duty to protect their charges. Weeks later, when it was finally safe for the children to come back, Monsieur Bohny went to retrieve them. One of the farmers denied that he had a child hidden there. But sure enough, the next day, that very girl showed up at the Swiss Aid home where she belonged. The farmer, who had never met Monsieur Bohny before, wanted to be sure the girl would be safe. He hadn't wanted to hand the girl over to someone he didn't know.

One day in 1944, a woman claiming to be a journalist came to L'Abric to speak to Monsieur Bohny. She said she was writing an article on Swiss Aid for Children and wanted to ask him some questions. They talked, then she asked if he had any information on the *maquis*—Resistance fighters. Monsieur Bohny told her firmly that since he was a representative of the Swiss Red Cross and Swiss Aid for Children, he had no contact with the maquis. However, he realized that she was hoping he would put her in contact with them. He knew that some of the counselors at the Swiss Aid homes were close to the maquis. After she left, he told the counselors about her. They did just what he had hoped they would. They went to the maquis to tell them about the woman, and then the maquis contacted her.

It turned out that the woman was not a journalist. She was an American named Virginia Hall, and she became an important member of the Resistance. She helped the maquis get weapons from the Allies for the 850 resistance fighters of the region. Without those weapons, they would never have been able to defend themselves. Monsieur Bohny had found a perfect solution—he helped the maquis without endangering the children in his care. After the war, he received a letter from one of the heads of the maquis thanking him for what he had done.

August Bohny met his wife, Friedel Reiter, during the war. She was a nurse and worked for Swiss Aid for Children as well, in the Rivesaltes internment camp. They met when she brought some children from Rivesaltes to a Swiss Aid home. Later, she came to Le Chambon to work with Monsieur Bohny there. They married right after the war.

August Bohny and Friedel Reiter, with some interned children, stand at the door of the Swiss Aid barrack in the Rivesaltes internment camp.

L'Abric, the Swiss Aid home where Nathalie lived in Le Chambon

CHAPTER EIGHT

Waiting for a Letter
Nathalie

NATHALIE WAS BORN IN 1929 *in Antwerp, Belgium. When she was a child, her family moved to Paris, France. She was ten or eleven years old when the German army invaded France, and she went to Le Chambon when she was twelve or thirteen. She was fifteen or sixteen years old in 1945, when the Allies achieved victory in Europe. She told us her story at her home in Créteil, France, when we interviewed her on November 8, 2002, and again on April 3, 2004.*

Age 9 or 10—Autumn 1939, Paris, France

We're leaving Paris. Mama says we're going to Agen. My aunt and uncle live near there, in the countryside. Papa can't come with us. Before the war he was a doctor, but now he's an officer in the army, so he has to fight. It's just Mama, me, and my little sister, Anita. We're going to the south. Papa says we will be safer there.

Age 10 or 11—1940, Agen, France

Germany has taken over France! Papa is home now, but he's not allowed to work as a doctor anymore. The government says no Jews can practice medicine.

Age 12 or 13—June 1942, Agen, France

One day last week, when I was walking to school, the postman's wife leaned out her window and said to me urgently, "Tell your parents that tonight something's going to happen." I ran home and told Mama. That night we slept at my aunt and uncle's house, out in the country. This morning, the postman's wife told me the same thing again.

I'm not sure why she's warning us, but I think it has something to do with us being Jewish. Or maybe it's because Mama and Papa are from Russia, and I was born in Belgium. In our family, only my little sister, Anita, was actually born in France.

I'M GOING TO A VACATION CAMP! It's in the mountains in a place called Le Chambon. I get to stay until school starts in September.

Age 12 or 13—July 1942, Le Chambon-sur-Lignon, France

A lot of kids came on the train together, all of us without our parents. We're all staying in one of the three Swiss Aid for Children homes. The first house, Faïdoli, is for little kids. I'm in L'Abric. And then there's La Guespy, for the older kids. Monsieur Bohny is the director of all three houses, but he lives in L'Abric with us. All the kids call him Papa Gusti.

Age 12 or 13—August 1942, Le Chambon-sur-Lignon, France

Every morning, we salute the two flags: Swiss and French. Everyone shares in the chores, and we go hiking and play games. The food is wonderful—we even

Papa Gusti at the piano with Friedel Reiter, his fiancée

get chocolate and jam—and after dinner, Papa Gusti plays the piano and we all sing songs. Sometimes there are skits, or someone gets up and tells a story. It's a lot of fun.

I GOT A LETTER! Mama and Papa say they are fine and they hope I'm having a good time. I am! Tonight when Papa Gusti kissed us all good night, I told him about my letter.

Age 12 or 13—September 1942, Le Chambon-sur-Lignon, France

Why haven't Mama and Papa sent for me? School has started already.

Papa Gusti enrolled me in the Ecole Nouvelle Cévenole, the private school here in Le Chambon. I've already started classes. Why haven't I heard from Mama and Papa?

Age 13 or 14—January 1943, Le Chambon-sur-Lignon, France

Every day when they hand out the mail, I look for a letter. There never is one for me. I guess Mama and Papa don't want me back. I don't understand.

MOMO LIKES LINOU, and Vova likes Nany—that's me! Nany is short for Nathalie. Nobody but my family ever called me Nany before, but everyone here calls me that.

We four do everything together: We talk, we argue, we get mad at one another, we laugh, everything. We're all the same age, and we're best friends.

Vova is Russian. He's a real troublemaker, but he plays the piano wonderfully. I hear him practice every morning, and the music flows over me. I can see why Momo likes Linou so much. She's such a flirt, and she's small and slim and very smart.

ALL THE KIDS IN L'ABRIC are divided into four teams: the Lions, the Tigers, the Eagles, and the Squirrels. Momo, Vova, Linou, and I are Tigers. The teams take turns each week doing different chores: cooking, serving meals, sweeping,

Doing chores: three girls in Le Chambon carrying milk cans

mending, laundry, and shopping. We help the grown-ups, the counselors, the cook, and the housekeeper. I like it, because all the time while we're peeling potatoes or running errands we're also cracking jokes and laughing.

One time, just for fun, Papa Gusti announced that the cook and the housekeeper and all the other adults would have the day off, and the kids would do all the work. Someone had read about a festival in the Roman Empire, where the masters served the slaves. That day, the grown-ups had their Roman holiday. They all slept late, and we did everything. It went very well. I guess we've learned a lot more than we realized about housework!

PAPA GUSTI FOUND ME SOME woolen trousers. It's very cold here, and we have to wear many layers of clothing to keep warm. I had no winter clothes of my own, and I've outgrown all the clothes I brought with me to Le Chambon. Whenever we outgrow our things, we pass them on to other kids. Whatever fits, we wear. I'm wearing clothes handed down from some of the older kids. All the girls wear pants. It's much more practical in the snow.

The snow is really deep now. We use wooden snowshoes to get around. The other kids go sledding and skiing, but not me. I don't like sports.

This week it's the Tigers' turn to take the cart into town for food. Momo, Linou, Vova, and I are going. It isn't easy in the snow, but it's still fun. We get to wander around the village, visiting merchants and picking up provisions for the house. There are around forty of us living in L'Abric, and the basement is full of shelves to hold food. The cart is very heavy coming back, and when we go up the hill, it always takes two of us to pull and two of us to push.

Age 13 or 14—Summer 1943, Le Chambon-sur-Lignon, France

I still look for a letter from Mama and Papa every day. Some kids get lots of mail, but I don't get any. I think my parents have forgotten me.

I've been here a whole year. Other kids come and go. Sometimes they leave in the middle of the night. No one tells us where they've gone, but we hear things. We know that some kids have been secretly sent to Switzerland. Some of the kids will go back home. Others don't have any family to go back to. My friend Hélène came here after her mother and father were arrested.

In Le Chambon it hardly feels like there's a war going on. But there are kids here who have come from all over and have been horribly affected by the war. One night, they brought in a very young Greek girl. She was sitting in the kitchen. She was very pale and didn't say a word. Someone handed her a glass of milk, and she reacted as though he were going to hit her. Later I found out that both of her parents had been shot right in front of her. She was so terrified, she slept with her eyes wide open every night. She didn't stay here very long.

When kids come from the internment camps, they are always very thin and their skin is as dry as a snake. Marcel, the little Spanish boy, came from a camp. He was terribly skinny, he had hardly any hair, and his eyes kept oozing.

JEAN IS MY FAVORITE COUNSELOR. He was studying to be a doctor when he and his fiancée were arrested by the *gendarmes*—police. She was sent away on a train, and they beat him for seventeen hours straight. He survived, and they released him, and he came here to hide. He's Jewish like me.

The kids here don't care who's Jewish and who isn't, but I know Vova, Linou, and Momo aren't Jewish, and Hélène is.

Jean said that what had happened to him could happen to anybody, even me. He showed me the secret of how he survived. He told me to tighten the muscles in my arm, and he hit me there. It hurt! Then he said to make my arm go limp, and he hit me again. That time, my arm gave way, and it didn't hurt. He told me if you relax your muscles like that, you can last a long time.

Age 13 or 14—Autumn 1943, Le Chambon-sur-Lignon, France

This is not a game. It's the middle of the night. They woke us up and told us to get dressed. They said we were going on a hike. Not all of us, like when we go hiking during the day—Momo and Linou and Vova are not here, but Hélène is.

Now we're walking through the woods. I'm not quite awake yet, and it's dark, but I'm with friends. We know we're hiding, and that's scary. But we're together, and the counselors are with us. I wonder how long we'll be out here, and what will happen next.

THE SUN IS COMING UP. From this hillside, through the trees, we can see the flagpole in front of L'Abric. Papa Gusti is raising the flags. The Swiss flag is above the French flag. The counselors tell us that that means it's safe to come back. If he had raised the French flag first, we would have had to stay out here longer.

Age 14 or 15—Spring 1944, Le Chambon-sur-Lignon, France

School is great. Boys and girls are together in class. Before I came to Le Chambon, I was always in school with just girls. I like it that everyone works really hard. We take our studies seriously, and all the kids are smart.

Our teachers are never boring, and class is quite exciting. The German teacher is from Austria; the English teacher is English. I love my literature professor, because he really listens to us, and he lets us borrow his books. I'm becoming a real bookworm.

Age 14 or 15—Autumn 1944, Le Chambon-sur-Lignon, France

It's been over two years since I got that letter from Mama and Papa. Nothing since then. I suppose I'll never see my family again. My life is here now.

Age 15 or 16—January 1945, Le Chambon-sur-Lignon, France

The grown-ups here in L'Abric are pretty strict about following the rules, but we kids know how to get around them. We're very well organized, and we look out for each other. That's why I'm sitting here in bed, eating chocolate. I got in big trouble, and the counselor sent me to bed without dessert. I was fuming. When no one was looking, Momo and Linou snuck up here with some chocolate for me. It's delicious!

Age 15 or 16—Spring 1945, Le Chambon-sur-Lignon, France

I just learned something sad about the cook. She's Russian, and she and her children live here at L'Abric. We all like her. We found out that her husband killed himself to protect them. He was Jewish and they're not. When all the anti-Jewish laws appeared, he thought that his family was in danger because of him, and he threw himself in front of a train. Now she has to take care of their children all by herself.

Age 15 or 16—May 1945, Le Chambon-sur-Lignon, France

I have to leave. Papa Gusti told me after dinner. Mama and Papa have sent for me! I'll be here until the end of school, two more months. The war is over and everyone is leaving. But I've gotten used to living here.

Age 15 or 16—July 1945, Agen, France

I'm looking out the train window. We're pulling into the station at Agen. I can't wait to see my family! It's been three years.

I grab my things and step down onto the platform. And then I see them, Mama and Papa and Anita, waiting for me! They look so different. Something has changed, or maybe I've changed.

Age 15 or 16—August 1945, Agen, France

I miss all my friends from L'Abric. It's so odd to be living with just three other people. It's boring and quiet. I have no friends here at all. I know Mama and Papa love me, and I love them, but they just don't understand. I feel like a grown-up, but they treat me like a child, always telling me what to do. What am I doing here?

Age 15 or 16—October 1945, Agen, France

I hate school. The teachers are boring. In Le Chambon, I was a good student. Here I'm a genius compared to the other girls. Everybody's so dumb here. I don't like being back in a school with all girls, either.

Nobody will talk to me. I don't fit in at all. I'm the only girl in Agen who wears trousers. I got used to wearing them in Le Chambon. They're very practical and I wear them all the time. What's wrong with that?

Now I know why Mama and Papa never wrote to me. It was too dangerous. We could all have been arrested because we're Jewish, and also because Mama and Papa and I were born outside of France. So Mama and Papa left me in Le Chambon for all that time. They got forged identity papers for my sister, Anita, and they sent her to live with some farmers until the end of the war.

One day, after I left, the postman's wife warned Mama and Papa that she had heard there would be a roundup that night. Mama went to Madame Galiciolli, an Italian woman who has a little shop downtown selling seeds and beans to the farmers. Mama said to her, "My husband and I would like to spend some time in the countryside. . . . Do you know someone who could lodge us? We could leave today." Mama was hoping the woman would know of somewhere safe for them to stay, but she didn't want to be too obvious. Madame Galiciolli talked to her husband and came back and said, "We'll take care of you."

Mama and Papa ended up spending a whole year hiding in a small room downtown that was owned by the Galiciollis. They never once went outside. The three Galiciolli boys brought Mama and Papa food every day, and in exchange, Papa helped them with their lessons. Afterward, Mama found out that the reason Madame Galiciolli had helped them was because she thought Mama looked just like the Italian queen!

Age 16 or 17—1946, Agen, France

My mother gave me a set of paints for my sixteenth birthday. I didn't know what to do with it. I'd never painted before, and I didn't even try, at first. But I couldn't just set it aside, because it was a gift from Mama. You can't just throw out a gift from someone you love.

I decided to take it with me when we went on vacation. I got it out and started painting. It was difficult! But it was also exciting. I keep coming back to it. Usually when I try something new, it's easy for me, and sometimes that gets boring. But this is different.

EPILOGUE

Nathalie Stern became an artist. She went on to exhibit her paintings, prints, and collages in galleries in France. She continues to do her art today, in her studio in a suburb of Paris.

When she was seventeen years old, Nathalie learned that the man she knew as her father was actually her stepfather. Her mother had remarried when Nathalie was very young, and she never knew her biological father, who was Polish. Her stepfather had French citizenship, and when her mother married him, that gave her French citizenship as well. Nathalie was the only member of her family who was not considered a French citizen. This put her in greater danger during the war. She went to Le Chambon because the Protestant pastor of Agen had come to her parents and suggested that Nathalie be sent to one of the Swiss Aid houses there, where she would be safe.

One day, when Nathalie was seventy years old, she received a phone call from someone who called her by her nickname, Nany. No one outside her immediate family had used that name since she left Le Chambon. It was Papa Gusti—Monsieur Bohny—call-

ing her from the Paris airport, between flights. She went to meet him there. They hadn't seen each other in fifty-five years! It was a joyful reunion.

Nathalie says, "[L'Abric] was very lively, it was very gay! I mean, it wasn't a sad place. . . . There were the mountains, there was the snow, there was sledding, it was cold! . . . And it was such a mix, that's important! Young and old, boys and girls, doing chores, making mischief, singing songs."

She adds, "Almost everyone [in Le Chambon] was quietly, silently, without saying a word, busy protecting people who were threatened. And children aren't aware of this sort of thing. . . . It's funny to think that your life has been saved without you even knowing it at the time."

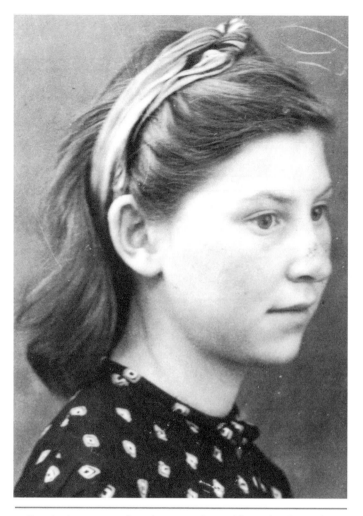

Erna in June 1942, after she was released from the Rivesaltes internment camp

CHAPTER NINE

Afraid to Say Hello
Erna

ERNA WAS BORN IN NÜRNBERG, *Germany, on December 21, 1925. She was thirteen years old when Hitler's army invaded Poland, and World War II began. She came to Le Chambon when she was sixteen, and she was nineteen when the Allies achieved victory in Europe in 1945. She told us her story in a letter and a follow-up telephone conversation in 2004.*

IN 1940, ERNA AND HER MOTHER were deported from Mannheim, Germany, along with all the other Jewish people from Baden and the Palatinate, two provinces in Germany. Her father had passed away five years earlier. Erna and her mother were sent to the Gurs internment camp in France. Erna was fourteen years old.

After several months in Gurs, they were transferred to the Rivesaltes internment

Women and children trying to stay warm in a barrack at the
Rivesaltes internment camp

camp. Her mother was ill and very weak from the harsh conditions at Gurs. By the
time they got to Rivesaltes, she was so ill, she didn't even recognize her own daughter.

Friedel Reiter, a nurse with Swiss Aid for Children who worked in the camp,
sent Erna's mother to Elne. There was a maternity hospital there that would take in
sick women from Rivesaltes, when they had the space. Erna was released from
Rivesaltes at the same time.

She stayed for two months at a home run by the Jewish Scouts of France. After

Erna's real identity card from Germany, with the big *J* for "Jude"—Jewish—stamped on it. Other rules for the IDs of Jews: The left ear had to be showing in the picture, and "Sara" or "Israel" had to be added as the person's middle name.

that, she was hidden by a French family in their home. While she was there, she was given a false identification card. Her new name was Eveline Hebert. Her identification card said that she was from Alsace, a region in France. In fact, she had never been to Alsace, and she spoke very poor French!

Erna was unable to find a safe place to hide. Eventually, determined to see her mother again, she came back to the hospital in Elne. The hospital director kindly let her stay for several months. Erna helped to take care of the newborn babies and the toddlers. She was thrilled to be reunited with her mother. Erna was able to stay until her mother had to return to Gurs in the winter of 1943.

Erna was lucky that she didn't have to go back to an internment camp. The hospital director in Elne found a place for her in Le Chambon. She was hired as a *lingère*—a laundress—in L'Abric, one of the Swiss Aid homes. Erna didn't mind having to work. She was simply grateful to have a roof over her head and food in her stomach.

L'Abric was run by August Bohny, with the help of Mademoiselle Reiter, who had come from Rivesaltes to work there with him. Erna was only eighteen years old at the time. Some of the children living at L'Abric were older than she was!

It was Erna's job to wash and iron all of the children's clothing. But she spent much of her time mending worn clothing and letting out the seams when things became too short or too small for all those growing kids! In her spare time, she helped in the kitchen or cleaned the house. Everybody pitched in wherever they could.

Erna had studied English at school in Germany for four years, so she helped the kids at L'Abric with their English homework. At night, she would borrow their English textbooks. She told them that she wanted to use the books to prepare their next tutoring session. Actually, she was using the books to teach herself French. She used her second language—English—to teach herself a third language—French!

One day, when she was running an errand in the village, Erna saw an old friend of hers from Germany. Neither of them spoke. They didn't know each other's false names, and they were both afraid that someone on the street would overhear them talking and figure out that they were Jews in hiding. They were afraid to even say hello! Erna and her friend had been deported from Germany at the same time, and had been in the same internment camps, but they couldn't say a word to each other.

Epilogue

Erna Heymann stayed in Le Chambon until the end of the war, when she was reunited with her mother. She had an older sister who had become a U.S. citizen in 1944. Erna and her mother joined her in the United States in 1946.

Erna married a fellow German whom she met in Ohio. They settled there. Erna Heymann Bernstein has three children and six grandchildren.

Erna kept in touch with Friedel Reiter and August Bohny. She says, "I most certainly do remember him [August Bohny] as a very kind, warm, sensitive, and helpful person. . . . Being sheltered by the Bohnys was the most important thing for me."

This photo, taken in June 1944, includes, from left, Pastor Trocmé (with his son Jacques), Pastor Theis, Mireille Philip, Madeleine Barot, and Pastor Jacques Martin. All five risked their own lives to save the lives of Jewish refugees on the plateau.

CHAPTER TEN

Escape to Switzerland

FOR REFUGEES, ESPECIALLY THOSE who needed to flee to Switzerland, Mireille Philip was one of the most important people on the plateau. Some people referred to her as "The Boss." She was in the Resistance and helped acquire blank forms to use in making false papers—some of them were parachuted in. She also helped to make false papers. Forged stamps for the papers were carved into the bottoms of spools of thread, which were hidden, casually tossed into her sewing basket.

Madame Philip and Pastor Theis established Le Chambon as the starting point for an escape route to Switzerland. Many refugees came to La Montagne Protestante with the express purpose of continuing on to Switzerland, rather than to stay hidden there. In making arrangements, Madame Philip sometimes had to go to Switzerland herself. But this was very dangerous. She would disguise herself as a man and work

The farms of the plateau, many of them quite isolated, made good hiding places for refugees.

on a locomotive, shoveling coal from St. Etienne to Geneva. She'd arrive in Switzerland covered head to toe in black coal dust!

Pierre Piton, a student at the Ecole Nouvelle Cévenole, was one of the people who worked with Madame Philip. The refugees would arrive in Le Chambon and immediately be hidden in someone's home nearby. Pierre would talk to farmers in the neighboring area to make arrangements. Then, in the middle of the night, he would take his sled and pick up two or three of the refugees at a time. Carrying their meager belongings on his sled, he would lead them to one of the farms on the plateau, where they were to be hidden. They would remain there while Madame Philip obtained the false papers they needed. Roger Darcissac, the head of the public school, took photos of the refugees. Pastor Theis made them false identity cards, as did others on the plateau. Madame Philip made arrangements for the refugees to remain legally in Switzerland—if they made it there safely.

Many of the refugees didn't speak French. Before leaving for Switzerland, they would be given instructions for the journey in their own language. They were told not to speak, either to one another or to anyone else. They should pretend they didn't even know Pierre, who would be guiding them. On the train, when asked for their tickets, they should try to act naturally. They should avoid eye contact, and if anyone seemed to be watching them, they should pretend to be asleep.

Pierre would wear a Boy Scout uniform on the journey. He was only seventeen,

Paul Majola, a nine-year-old shepherd boy, delivered false papers. Oscar Rosowsky and Sammy Charles made false papers for Resistance fighters and refugees, from the shelter of Henri and Emma Héritier's farm. Oscar and Sammy hid the papers in an empty beehive and Monsieur Héritier's mother's grave. Paul picked up the papers and distributed them. [Chambon Foundation]

and had his own false identification card. Nobody paid much attention to a Boy Scout who seemed to be traveling alone.

It would take two days to reach the border of Switzerland. Late at night, Pierre would lead the refugees to the barbed-wire fence at the border. He would have them lie down in a ditch, waiting for the guards to go by. Once the guards were past, there would be a few minutes before the next patrol. As soon as the coast was clear, Pierre would signal, and, one by one, the refugees would slip under the barbed wire onto Swiss soil.

It would take Pierre two days to get back to Le Chambon. Exhausted, he would rest for a day or two. Then he would do it all over again, with three more refugees.

After making twenty such trips, and seeing sixty refugees safely into Switzerland, Pierre was caught twice and beaten by the police. He was very lucky—both times he was released shortly after being arrested. It was too dangerous then for him to continue as a guide, so someone else took his place.

Many other people guided refugees to Switzerland, often following very different routes. Some refugees climbed the Alps to get to Switzerland. Some swam across the border. (The shoreline of Lake Leman passes through both France and Switzerland.) Some attended fake funerals at a cemetery right on the border, and slipped over the wall during the service. Sometimes a fake soccer match in a field by the border would shield the people as they crossed into Switzerland.

There were numerous groups of people between La Montagne Protestante and Switzerland who cooperated to bring refugees to safety.

CIMADE (Comité Inter-Mouvements Auprès Des Evacués) was a French Protestant organization run by Madeleine Barot. CIMADE helped people in French internment camps, brought many of them to the plateau and other safe places, and also organized escape routes to Switzerland. The former mayor of Le Chambon, Charles Guillon, worked with CIMADE during the war, taking charge of the refugees once they were in Switzerland.

CIMADE set up a house on the plateau, Le Côteau Fleuri, for refugees who had been released from the camps. Madame Barot brought in Pastor Marc Donadille to help run it. Le Côteau Fleuri was a kind of way station. The refugees would stay there until CIMADE could guide them to safety into Switzerland.

One night, they received a warning that the *gendarmes*—police—were coming to arrest Jews. They had planned for this, and they had teams to take everyone to safe hiding places around the plateau. Three women refused to leave the house, because they were afraid, so they were hidden up in the attic. Another woman refused to hide, saying that she was not considered Jewish and that she was related to a high Nazi official. The gendarmes tried to arrest her, anyway. Suddenly, she had a seizure and fell to the floor, with her eyes rolled back. The doctor was called in immediately. When the gendarmes were looking away, she winked at Pastor Donadille! The doctor said that she was too ill to be transported, and the gendarmes left. Afterward, she told the pastor that she had used that trick before.

For the others, the safe hiding places worked, and only one person was arrested. A young girl, who had been hidden in a pastor's home, answered the door when a gendarme knocked. He told her to pack her bag while he waited for her on the doorstep. She didn't understand that he was actually giving her a chance to escape through the back door. When she reappeared with her suitcase, he had to arrest her. The poor girl perished in a Nazi concentration camp.

Jakob, third from left, with other boys in Le Chambon

CHAPTER ELEVEN

I'll Fight Back
Jakob

JAKOB WAS BORN IN WURZBURG, *Germany, on April 26, 1925. When Hitler came to power in Germany in 1933, Jakob was seven years old, and he was thirteen on* Kristall- nacht—*the Night of Broken Glass. Jakob came to Le Chambon when he was sixteen, along with Hanne, Joseph, and four other young refugees. He was twenty years old in 1945, when the Allies achieved victory in Europe. He told us his story in New York when we interviewed him on February 22, 2003, and on May 20, 2003.*

Age 10—1936, Frankfurt, Germany

I'm sick and tired of being bullied just because I'm Jewish. Before I started school, I was a happy kid. But now all the Nazi kids call me "Dirty Jew," and I come home from school bloody almost every day. I might not be the biggest, strongest kid in Germany, but I'm tough, and I know how to stick up for my-self. My brother, Martin, is eleven, a year older than I am, but I'm even tougher than he is. Martin and I used to do everything together, but last year my parents sent him to Berlin to stay with our aunt. Before they sent me to school in Frankfurt, Mutter [Mother] was worried about my fighting back. She said, "Look at you! You're going to get us all into jail yet." And I told her, "I don't care, I'll defend myself. This is my right!"

Frankfurt is a bigger city than Kleinlangheim, my hometown. My parents thought that I would be safer here in Frankfurt and wouldn't have to fight so much. But there are lots of Nazis here, too, and the kids like me that go to the *yeshiva*—religious school—have to wear *yarmulkes*—skullcaps. So now it's even easier for the Nazi kids to tell I'm Jewish. Yesterday, this guy took me out and beat the living hell out of me, and I went to school crying all the way. This morning, he was after another kid, but there were four of us together, and we threw him through a drugstore window. And then we ran! So far, today, no one else has bothered us.

Age 13—1938, Frankfurt, Germany

I've been in Frankfurt now for two years, and suddenly I have to go home. My parents say they can't afford to send me to school here anymore, because business is so bad. They're wine merchants. I'm not too sorry to leave. I don't mind going to school at home again. Besides, I miss Grosspapa [Grandpa] and Gross-mama [Grandma] a lot, and Mutter and Vater [Father], too. And when I get home I'll get to see my dog, Waldi.

Age 13—Kristallnacht, November 10, 1938, Kitzengen, Germany

Something is going on. I don't know what it is, but I'm scared. On the way to school this morning, I could see a big fire from the train window. All the other kids were shouting, "Oh, wonderful! The synagogue is burning. Oh, those dirty Jews!" How dare they say that!

The synagogue in Aachen, Germany, after being destroyed on
Kristallnacht. All over Germany, the Nazis targeted Jews and Jewish
property on the night of November 9, 1938, and the following day.
This came to be known as Kristallnacht.

I got off the train, but instead of going to school, I went to my aunt's house.
All the way there, I saw awful things: Storm Troopers were breaking windows,
beating people, and setting things on fire. People were running everywhere,
screaming and crying. My uncle was gone. My aunt told me that they had ar-

rested him and my other two uncles, and I'd better just stay with her. But I don't care what she says, I'm going home.

Age 13—November 10, 1938, Kleinlangheim, Germany

I snuck out and I went home the back way. My worst fears came true. Everything I had seen on the way home was happening to my family, too. My house was surrounded by Nazis, and all the windows had been broken. I could see Storm Troopers in the basement. They were breaking the wine casks that my parents were going to sell. Wine was pouring out onto the floor, and they were drinking as much as they could. I ran inside. I saw Mutter and Grosspapa and Grossmama, but where was Vater?

Mutter said to one of the Storm Troopers, "Somebody stole my winter coat." The Storm Trooper looked really angry, and shouted, "Everybody goes to jail!" They took me, too, and even my dog!

They took us to the city hall and made us wait. We didn't know what they were going to do to us. Mutter told me that they had arrested Vater that morning. She didn't know where they had taken him. After a while, they let me and my grandparents go. But they didn't give us back Waldi, and they said to Mutter, "You! Stay!"

Our house was in a shambles. The Storm Troopers had taken everything of value and destroyed everything else. A half hour later, Mutter came home. She was crying, and her mouth was bleeding. It was an awful sight. She told us that one of the Storm Troopers said to her, "A National Socialist [Nazi] does not steal!" and smashed her right in the face and knocked all her teeth out. He was the same one she had told about her winter coat.

That night we slept in the office upstairs. It was the only room that had any windows left. It was freezing in the house.

We're fixing the windows ourselves. The Nazis took our insurance money. We found out that they killed Waldi that day, and now they just won't leave us alone. We can't go to the bakery, we can't go anywhere. Some nice people who used to work for us come in the middle of the night and bring us food.

Vater finally came home yesterday after four weeks. He told us he was in Dachau, a concentration camp. The only reason they let him go was because he had been a soldier for Germany in the Great War. That's the only thing that saved him.

Age 14—1939, Berlin, Germany

I'm in Berlin with Martin. We both go to school here now, and we're living with my aunt. My parents think boys aged fourteen and fifteen are too young to live on their own. They had to sell our house, and the Nazis gave them twenty-four hours to leave Germany. They claimed that my parents had been hiding weapons in the house. My parents paid a smuggler to help them sneak across the border to Holland [the Netherlands], and from there they went to Belgium. Grosspapa and Grossmama stayed in Holland with a relative. I really miss them.

Martin and I get letters from my parents sometimes. They're in a refugee camp in the mountains called Marneffe. I miss them, too. Now that Germany has invaded Poland, and we are at war, things here are even more difficult. Martin and I have agreed that we can't stay in Germany anymore. We're going to try to get to Belgium.

Age 14—October 18, 1939, Belgium

We've seen a lot of smugglers in the past few days. Our great-uncle gave us the money to pay them. We crossed the border into Holland. All we brought with us was a change of clothes in our knapsacks, nothing else. We had to leave everything else behind. It was important that it look like we were only going away for the day, not leaving for good.

We met the first smugglers at the train station in Cologne. We were told that one of them would have a newspaper under his arm and that's how we would recognize him. He was a big, tall guy, with blue eyes. Really Aryan-looking. The two smugglers knew exactly where to take us and where the border guards would be. They knew just when it would be safe to cross the border. I asked them who they were. The tall guy said, "We are from the Gestapo," and he showed us his papers. It was true! They were the Nazi secret police! Why were they helping us? We didn't dare ask.

One of the smugglers drove us all the way through Holland. We were so close to Grosspapa and Grossmama, but we couldn't stop to see them. My heart broke. That night, a Dutch smuggler took us to the Belgian border. We were in a cemetery, but we weren't scared. He told us to climb over the back wall of the cemetery, and he would meet us on the other side. We made it! We're in Belgium!

Age 14—December 1939, near Liege, Belgium

We turned ourselves in to the police in Brussels, and they put us in jail. That was the first time I ever ate nonkosher food. Martin wouldn't touch it, but I said, "I'm hungry, I'm eating." The judge sentenced us to join our parents in the refugee camp. That was exactly what we wanted! Mutter and Vater were so happy to see us when we finally joined them at the refugee camp. And the way we got there was by getting ourselves arrested!

Marneffe is up in the mountains in a beautiful old *château*—castle. There are lots of other Jewish refugees here, from Germany, Austria, and Czechoslovakia. My parents had been very worried about us. It's wonderful to be together again.

Everybody here works. Vater works in the kitchen. Mutter knits socks for the army. And Martin and I are working in the carpentry shop, but I'm not very good at it. Last month, I hit my hand with a hammer, and then when I was painting, some paint got into the cut. I got blood poisoning and it spread up my arm in three red stripes. It hurt. They were going to amputate my arm, but a doctor there, one of the Jewish refugees, said, "Let's try it without amputating the arm." Vater stayed next to me day and night, putting compresses on my arm. I was lucky to survive.

Age 15—May 10, 1940, Belgium

The director of the camp has just told us we have to leave. The Germans are invading Holland, France, and Belgium. He said, "We are being bombed by the Germans and we have to be evacuated. We'd better start marching toward France." We can't take much with us because we have to walk, so each of us has only one small suitcase. Not that we have very much to bring with us, anyway.

It's very hot today, and we have no water as we walk and walk. Bombs fall all around us, and we have to run and hide when the Stukas fly over us and strafe us with their machine guns. We are all terrified. As we walk, we see the French and British armies retreating.

Age 15—May 1940, Belgium and France

We're under arrest. The French Army has arrested our whole group. They think we are fifth column—German spies—just because we're German. They took us to army barracks in Charleroi, near the French border. They took Mutter away. We don't know where she is. Then they put us in cattle wagons and shipped us to a camp in France called Le Vigiant. Now they want to machine-gun us as spies. But we have a rabbi with us, and he is pleading for our lives.

Age 15—May 1940, Le Vigiant camp, France

Thank goodness the commander of this camp is a Moroccan Jew. The rabbi has managed to convince him that we're not spies, but mostly Jewish refugees, so they won't shoot us. Now Vater and Martin and I are being sent to an internment camp, again in cattle wagons. It's so hot out.

Age 15—July 1940, St. Cyprien internment camp, France

It was a long trip down here to the St. Cyprien internment camp—four days in the cattle wagons with no water and no food. St. Cyprien is right on the beach and it's very hot and full of sand fleas. We're living in tents and there's no escape from the heat. The food is terrible—Jerusalem artichokes swimming in water. We spend our time killing sand fleas.

The Gurs internment camp

Age 15—October 1940, Gurs internment camp, France

I thought St. Cyprien was bad, but it's nothing compared to Gurs. The only good thing about this place is that we found Mutter here. Of course, she's in the women's section, so we don't get to see her very often. Gurs is an internment camp in southwest France, and it's the most disgusting place I've ever seen. When it rains you sink up to your ankles in the mud, and there are rats everywhere. People are starving here. They give us carrots cut up and boiled in water, with maybe a little hunk of meat in it. A piece of bread, always either too wet or too hard. And never enough. Swiss Aid for Children gives us kids halvah, powdered milk, and processed cheese, but we have to take turns because there is not enough for everyone. I'm down to ninety pounds.

Everybody here has lice, which is why Vater and I have set up a little business. We boil people's clothing in big garbage cans to kill the louse eggs. It's really hard for me to lift the cans, though, so I'm going to ask to work in the infirmary instead. Martin and Mutter both just got back from eight weeks in the hospital with typhoid. I'm so relieved that they are better.

Last night, a woman from a children's aid organization, Oeuvre de Secours aux Enfants, called OSE, asked my parents if they wanted to send me to a village somewhere in France where I could stay in a home for refugee teenagers run by Swiss Aid for Children. She said I would be much safer there. They can only take kids who are sixteen and younger, so I just made it. Maybe Martin can come later. It will really be hard to leave my family behind.

Age 16—September 1941, France

I'm traveling with six other kids: Hanne (*see* Chapter Twenty-six, "Love in Wartime: Hanne and Max"), Lilli, Mannfred, Willi, and the twins, Joseph (*see* Chapter Twenty-five, "The Bad Boy of La Guespy: Joseph") and Victor. We're all close to the same age. None of them are my friends from the camp, but I know them by sight. We're becoming friends now. I'm glad not to have to travel alone.

Age 16—November 1941, Le Chambon-sur-Lignon, France

I'm in Le Chambon-sur-Lignon. It's way up on a high plateau in the mountains. It's beautiful here. What a difference from Gurs! I'm staying at La Guespy, which is a home for refugee kids like me. Lots of the kids are Jewish, but not all of them. Hanne and the others I came with are all staying here, too. Monsieur Bohny is head of all three Swiss Aid homes for refugee kids in Le Chambon. The lady who is in charge of us here at La Guespy is named Mademoiselle Usach. She never smiles. What a grouch! None of us like her.

So far I've learned a few words of French. I have a nice teacher. Most of us

The seven young refugees who came to Le Chambon from Gurs together, posing in front of La Guespy with the director, Mademoiselle Usach. They are, from left, Joseph (see Chapter Twenty-five, "The Bad Boy of La Guespy: Joseph"), Jakob, Victor, Lilli, Mannfred, Hanne (see Chapter Twenty-six, "Love in Wartime: Hanne and Max"), and Willi.

don't know French. A nice Austrian refugee named Elisabeth (*see* Chapter Four, "Lost: Elisabeth"), who speaks perfect French, is helping us communicate with the people here. She's only a little older than us.

Age 16—February 1942, Le Chambon-sur-Lignon, France

I'm not going to school, so I help out in the kitchen here. I help cook potatoes, when we have them. And sometimes I go down to the village and shop for food. I do cleanup work and fool around with the other kids. Now that there's snow, we make trains with the sleds and go down the hill. It's a lot of fun. The snow is really deep.

The *gendarmes*—police—haven't come to round up Jews for a while because the roads are blocked by snow. It must be at least five feet deep. I'm glad we don't have to worry right now about roundups. But someone must be looking out for us because Monsieur Bohny always seems to know when there is going to be a roundup, and he sends all of us Jewish kids into the woods to hide until the gendarmes have gone.

This place is practically paradise, except for the roundups.

Age 17—September 1942, Le Chambon-sur-Lignon, France

I'm so glad Martin is here with me now. We're in hiding. We can't even go to the window and look out unless we make sure to stay behind the curtains so no one will see us. We can see the gendarmes marching back and forth on the street below. We're on the top floor of Madame Rivière's house, and we've been here for four weeks.

We almost got arrested. One night, the gendarmes came for all of us and Monsieur Bohny talked them out of arresting us. But they said they would be back, so we've been in hiding ever since. And they've been looking for us. We don't know where Hanne, Mannfred, Lilli, and everyone else is. They're spread out all over the plateau, on farms and in people's homes.

It's Martin and me and my friend Walter hiding here. Mostly we sit around and play cards. After school, René Rivière (*see* Chapter Twenty-three, "A Family in the Resistance: René") and his cousin Hélène Veillith and Jacques Rousseau come home. They're really nice. Jacques and his mother, Madame Rousseau, are staying here, too. They're friends of the Rivières.

Altogether, we're six kids and two adults. That's a lot of people to feed, and the three of us who are hiding don't have ration cards for food. René and Jacques have been catching frogs, so we've been eating a lot of frogs' legs. The baker brings bread on the quiet, at night. The farmers bring eggs. There's always something to eat. I think the farmers must know where all of us are hiding. Everyone here is looking out for us.

We're lucky because there's a shortwave radio in the house and we get news from Britain. It's in French, and we understand enough French now to know what they're saying. We think they're sending coded messages to the Resistance here in France. It's very exciting! We have newspapers here, too, so for the first time since we've been in Le Chambon, we can follow the news of the war. Usually, at La Guespy, we have no idea what's going on in the world. I wonder how Mutter and Vater are.

THE GENDARMES FINALLY LEFT. Thank goodness this roundup is over, and we can go back to La Guespy. It'll be great to see everyone again, except Mademoiselle Usach. And I can go visit Madame Philip again. She's so nice, and she reminds me of Mutter.

Age 17—September 1942, Le Chambon-sur-Lignon, France

Mutter and Vater are gone. They took everyone away. Hanne just got back from Gurs. She got permission to go there to visit her mother. When she got there, they were deporting everyone. We don't know where they are taking them. Somewhere in Germany or Poland. For the first time, I broke down. We're all consoling each other, the seven of us who came from Gurs together, and my brother. All our parents were there. Hanne said she saw her mother for an hour that morning through the fence, and then they put them all on cattle wagons. And now they're gone.

Age 17—January 1943, Le Chambon-sur-Lignon, France

Martin and I are working in the new carpentry shop now. I don't really like carpentry, but at least I know how to do it. We wear *sabots*—wooden clogs. That's what everyone wears in Le Chambon, and I've outgrown my old shoes. Yesterday, Martin and I snuck into the barn of that farm near La Guespy. There's a big hunk of bacon in there. We cut a piece off and ate it. It was delicious. The farmer's really nice—he's the one with the big mustache. I'm sure he knew we were there, but he didn't say a word.

Age 17—February 1943, Le Chambon-sur-Lignon, France

There was no warning this time. Martin and I have been arrested. That horrible man came into the carpentry shop and pointed his finger at me and said, "Finally got you!" Now we're sitting on the bus the gendarmes brought to carry away any Jews they could find. They've found fifteen or twenty of us so far. The people here don't want us to leave. They've gathered around the bus, singing *"Faut–il Nous Quitter Sans Espoir."* The song says they hope to see us again soon. Now they're lying on the ground around the bus. They're trying to stop the gendarmes from taking us away. A minute ago, a boy got on the bus and handed me a piece of chocolate. Then he turned and left. I don't even know him, but he gave me his chocolate!

They're starting the bus. They say they're taking us to Le Puy, which is where the Nazis are. I'm scared.

Age 17—February 1943, Le Puy-en-Velay, France

The gendarmes have interrogated me and so have the Germans. I'm really lucky. For some reason, they've decided to let me go. But not Martin. There's nothing I can do.

Age 17—March 1943, Le Chambon-sur-Lignon, France

I'm going. I can't stay here anymore. I've been in hiding near Le Chambon ever since the gendarmes released me. I'm on a farm run by the Salvation Army. There are other kids here, but I miss Martin an awful lot. I wonder where he is.

I work in the kitchen, and do what I can to help out. The people here are nice and the food is good, but I just can't stay here any longer. Tomorrow I'm going to Madame Philip. I love her and admire her so much, and she's always been so kind to me. Her husband is fighting the Germans with [Charles] de Gaulle in Algiers. Maybe she can help me get out of France.

I went to Madame Philip and I said, "I would like to go to Algiers. I want to join de Gaulle. I want to fight." But she said, "No, you're going to Switzerland!"

Switzerland is a neutral country in the war, so Jews are safe from the Nazis there. Madame Philip sent me to Pastor Theis, and he made me up some false papers. He had the stamps and some authentic forms. Madame Philip and I sat at his dining-room table and watched him make a French *carte d'identité*—identity card—and a Boy Scout identification card. He took the picture off my German identification card that had the big *J* for Jewish on it, and he put the photo on my new ID. He had to make sure that the swastika came off. My new name is Jacques Levet, and it says on my ID card that I was born in Alsace-Lorraine. That's close to the German border, so it might explain my German accent if I'm stopped. Pastor Theis says I can leave for Switzerland in a couple of days.

Age 17—April 1943, France

I'm trying so hard not to laugh. I can't even smile, because then the German soldiers sitting on the train all around me will realize that I understand their jokes. I'm not supposed to understand German—I'm supposed to be a French Boy Scout just sitting here on the train going to Annecy. So I'd better not laugh at their jokes, even though they're really funny.

I left Le Chambon for Switzerland right after getting my false papers. They gave me a Boy Scout uniform to wear. That was my disguise. I had been in the Boy Scouts while I was in Le Chambon, but I didn't have a uniform—they were too expensive. Jean-Pierre, Pastor Trocmé's son, and Marco Darcissac, the son of the schoolmaster, took me by bicycle all the way down the mountains to Valence—seventy kilometers! I was scared stiff! I had never gone down such steep mountains before on a bike.

They left me with a lady in Valence. She took me to her brother, who was a pastor. I stayed for the whole weekend, and I even went to church with them! On Monday, another pastor came and we got on the train for Annecy, which is close to Switzerland.

Jakob, disguised as a French Boy Scout, ready to leave for Switzerland

The train is stopping. I reach up for my knapsack, and one of the German soldiers helps me with it! If he only knew who I really was!

Age 18—April 1943, France and Switzerland

From Annecy, the pastor and I went to Annemasse, very close to the Swiss border. We stayed over at a monastery, and late the next night, a smuggler—I think he was a monk—took us right up to the border. We had to hide for a while because of the police dogs. My heart was pounding. When it was quiet, the monk took us across the border. He gave us some Swiss money, and we took a trolley car into Geneva, where somebody else was waiting for us. I thought the pastor would go back to France, but he told me that he was a refugee, too, because he had spoken out in his church against the Nazis. We both turned ourselves in to the Swiss police.

Now I'm in a Swiss quarantine camp for refugees, but it's nothing like the camps in France. It's a hotel, and it's beautiful, and I'm safe here. I miss Martin and my whole family a lot, and all my friends in Le Chambon. I'm sure I'll make friends here, but for now, I'm really on my own. Yesterday was my birthday—I just turned eighteen.

EPILOGUE

Jakob Lewin (now known as Jack) was reunited with his brother, Martin, in Switzerland. Martin had been sent back to Gurs, where he remained for some time, until he was allowed to return to Le Chambon. From there, he went to Switzerland in much the same way as Jack.

Over the next three years, Jack worked as a cook in various refugee camps. He liked it so much that he asked to go to cooking school. The Swiss authorities enrolled him in a hotel school in Lucerne.

He and his brother learned that their parents, three grandparents, and most of their aunts and uncles had all perished in Nazi concentration camps. Their other grandfather had died just before being sent to a camp.

In 1946, the two brothers were sponsored by relatives to immigrate to the United States. Jack found work in the kitchen of a hotel in New York City.

In 1950, Jack joined the U.S. Army and was sent to Germany. He was not happy about being back there. After a stint in the army, he returned to his career as a chef in New York City. He is now retired.

He met his wife on a blind date. She was a nurse at a hospital in New York. A German Jew, she had escaped Nazi Germany on the Kindertransport. They have been married now for over fifty years and have three daughters and seven grandchildren. They live in New York.

When Jack was sixty-one years old, he attended a reunion in Le Chambon. At the end of the reunion, a tall man named Christian de Monbrison stood up and spoke to the group. He said that during the war, he had given his chocolate to a boy who had been arrested, and was sitting on a bus in the square in Le Chambon. He asked if anyone knew who that boy was. Jack told him, "That was me! I was that boy!"

Jack says when he was in hiding in Le Chambon, ". . . we had to make do with what we got. . . . We didn't go hungry, that's for sure."

He says of Le Chambon, "The farmers were very good to the Jews there."

Léon, about 1945, sitting on the wall outside their house, and Marthe, wearing sabots, standing by their house in 1944

CHAPTER TWELVE

Spies Next Door
Léon and Marthe

WE INTERVIEWED LÉON AND MARTHE, *natives of Le Chambon, in their hometown on November 11, 2002, and on April 5, 2004.*

LÉON AND HIS YOUNGER SISTER, Marthe, grew up on a farm outside of Le Chambon with their parents and their older sister, Lydie. At the beginning of the war, Léon was twelve years old and Marthe was only seven. The farm, called Les Versas, was very small. The family kept a few cows, pigs, hens, and rabbits, and they grew potatoes, wheat, and rye. The fields were not fenced in. They used a dog and a stick to keep the cows from roaming.

It was a long walk to school, more than a mile. After a breakfast of bread and coffee with milk, they would leave for school. Every day, they would come home for lunch—usually vegetables and rice, sometimes pork and potatoes. At the end of the school day, when they returned home, they'd have a snack of coffee with milk and a piece of bread. Dinner was usually soup and cheese. After dinner, they did their homework.

Everybody wore *sabots*—wooden clogs. Leather was scarce, because it had to be sent to Germany for the troops. The sabots were usually painted black, although the *sabotiers*—sabot makers—often painted children's sabots in bright colors. Marthe's were painted yellow.

At Christmastime, Léon went to Boy Scout camp on the plateau. The temperature was usually below zero. All the Scouts would sleep in the hay in a barn in the freezing cold. In the winter, Léon and Marthe often had time to get together with neighbors and play games. But in the summer, they would be much too busy helping their parents on the farm.

Léon knew that some of the other boys his age were Jewish. Marthe was younger, and although she knew that many of her classmates were foreigners, she didn't realize that some of them were Jewish. They all played together, and it was simply not something she thought about.

They also knew that strangers were staying in the upstairs apartment in their farmhouse, but they had no idea who they were or why they were there. Besides, they were used to having lodgers upstairs. During the summer holidays, their landlord rented the upstairs to vacationers. Léon and Marthe would hear their parents talking, and they would overhear bits of information, but no one told them that refugees were being sheltered there.

One winter day, the director of Marthe's school asked them to take a young Jewish boy to stay with their aunt and uncle, Eugènie and Samuel Héritier. The boy's parents had just been arrested in the Savoie and sent to an internment camp. Five-year-old Bubi had been brought to Le Chambon to be safe. Léon, Marthe, and their sister, Lydie, started walking with him through the snow. On the way, he got

The Chave family harvesting rye in 1945. Léon is standing behind his mother, and Marthe is on the end with their dog, Doly. Next to Marthe is their little lodger, Claudette. Their father is standing on top of the wagon.

very upset, threw himself to the ground, and said he had walked far enough for one day. He didn't want to walk any farther. Somehow they managed to get him to Les Versas, and Lydie put him on her bicycle and rode with him all the way to their aunt and uncle's house.

While Bubi lived with them, the Héritiers and a neighbor, Marie Brottes, sent packages to his parents at the internment camp where they were imprisoned. In the packages were letters full of news of Bubi and drawings that he had made for them.

When Bubi's mother and father were released, they came to Le Chambon. The family lived together there until the end of the war. Bubi's mother was a talented seamstress, and she was able to earn a living for them that way. She also taught Lydie how to sew.

Right next door to Léon and Marthe's farm was one of the most important people to work with the *maquis*—Resistance fighters—on the plateau, Virginia Hall. Léon and Marthe knew she was in the Resistance. They'd see her riding by on her bicycle, and they'd say to each other, "There she goes, off for another parachute drop." They could actually see the parachutes from their farm, as they fell from the sky.

Later, they found out that Virginia Hall used her bicycle to generate power for the radio transmitter she had hidden on the farm next door. They also discovered that many other Resistance fighters from as far away as Belgium had stayed there, right next door to them.

The parachutes could not be reused. Red-and-white pieces were given to Léon and Marthe's mother and she made clothing for the family out of them—shirts and dresses. The little girl next door had a beautiful white dress made from a parachute.

On June 6, 1944, Marthe went to school, as usual. But when she got there, she was told that there would be no school that day. The Allies had landed in Normandy. It was D-Day, a day to celebrate!

After D-Day, France became a battlefield again, as the Allies and the Resistance slowly pushed the Nazis out of France. Marthe's most frightening memory of life during wartime is of the German planes, during those last few months before Le Chambon was liberated. The planes would fly very close to the ground. When they were overhead, Marthe was sometimes even afraid to stay in her own house. The nearby village of St. Agrève was bombed by the Germans during that time. Once, Marthe asked a friend to come with her into the woods, because she felt it would be safer there, where no one could see them.

Léon saw the Allies' tanks and trucks come rolling through Le Chambon on

September 3, 1944. Everybody applauded and cheered. The war was finally coming to an end!

Today, Léon and Marthe Chave and their sister Lydie Chave-Russier all live in Le Chambon.

French soldiers, part of an armored division coming from North Africa, arrive in Le Chambon on September 3, 1944. [Chambon Foundation]

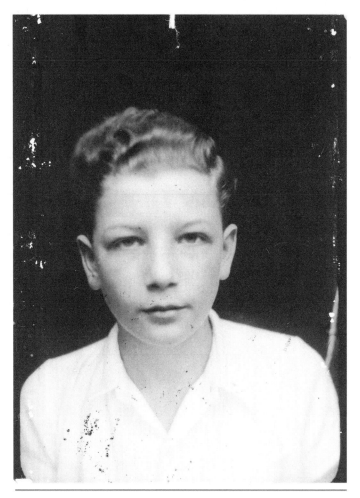

Henri, about ten years old

CHAPTER THIRTEEN

Living with Fear

Henri

HENRI WAS BORN IN BESANÇON, *France, on April 12, 1934. He was six years old when the Nazis invaded France, and he went to Le Chambon when he was nine. When the Allies achieved victory in Europe in 1945, he was eleven years old. He told us his story at his home in Oppedette, France, when we interviewed him on April 7, 2004.*

Age 6—Fall 1940, Montpellier, France

Ticktock, ticktock. My clock is broken, I'm just pretending. Papa sells clocks, and he gave me this alarm clock because it couldn't be fixed. I love to take it apart. Then I put it back together, and then I take it apart again. I brought it with me when we came here.

I know why we had to leave home, even though I'm only six. The Nazis

Henri's father

came, and we're afraid of the Nazis. Nazis don't like Jews. Mama and Papa told me, never tell anyone that you are a Jew.

I JUST BOUGHT A "MICKEY"! It's a Mickey Mouse magazine and it has lots of funny pictures.

Age 8—November 1942, Montpellier, France

The Nazis are coming to Montpellier. Mama and Papa and I have to leave. I'm scared.

Age 8—November 1942, La Tronche, France

Papa says it's better for us to be in La Tronche. Italian soldiers are in charge here, and they don't hate us as much as the Nazis do. I feel scared all the time, anyway.

Age 8—January 1943, La Tronche, France

The Nazis are here. They have taken over from the Italian soldiers. I'm so scared my stomach hurts.

Age 8—February 1943, Meylan, France

Mama and Papa and I are living in a house in the countryside near La Tronche. It's very cold in this house. We don't have a bathroom indoors, and we have to get all our water from the public fountain.

Henri's mother

We came here because it's not safe to stay in our apartment anymore. But the apartment is still our official home. That's the address on our identity cards. The Nazis would go looking for us there. But we would be here.

Mama goes into town every day to look for work doing sewing. She buys food with our ration cards and brings it here to Papa and me. Ever since we left Besançon, Papa hasn't had a job, and food is expensive. We don't have much.

Hardly anybody here knows we are Jewish. Papa told our landlady, because it is a crime to rent to Jews. He didn't want to lie to her. She said, "I don't want to know whether or not you are Jews!"

We don't wear the yellow star like we're supposed to. A new law says that we have to get *Juif*—"Jewish"—stamped on our identity cards, too. But a lady working in the town hall told us not to do it, so we didn't. Even so, I'm always afraid that somebody will find out about us.

Age 8—Spring 1943, Meylan, France

Papa has been working with the Resistance. I'm not sure what he does, but I think it's dangerous. Our landlady, Mademoiselle Pellissier, is in the Resistance, too, and they work together.

Papa was almost arrested today while I was at school. Mama was out working, so Papa was home all alone. He was studying his Hebrew books when German soldiers suddenly arrived. Mademoiselle Pellissier followed them in. They had just come from her house. She told them that he was her husband. The soldiers believed her, and they left without arresting him. They didn't even notice that his books were in Hebrew. Mademoiselle Pellissier saved Papa's life!

Age 9—May 1943, Meylan, France

I don't want to go to Switzerland. All I know about Switzerland is that it is the land of chocolate, whatever that means. Mama and Papa say they want me to go there to be safe. I want so badly to be safe, but I would really be scared to leave Mama and Papa.

Age 9—June 1943, Meylan, France

School is almost out. Mama and Papa want to send me to a vacation camp for the summer break. I've never been to a vacation camp before and I don't want to go.

The camp is in a place called Le Chambon. It is run by Swiss Aid for Children, and Mama and Papa say that they have good food at the camp. Maybe they will have chocolate. Papa says that he hopes they will send me to Switzerland from there, and I will be safe. I don't want to go without Mama and Papa. I'm afraid to take the train by myself. I'm afraid of the Nazis. I'm afraid of being alone.

Age 9—July 1943, en route to Le Chambon-sur-Lignon, France

Mama and Papa put me on the train this morning. I'm supposed to travel with some other kids. We're all going to Le Chambon, and everyone is around nine years old, like me. I'm the only Jew here. It's a good thing I'm with a group of Christians, because there are Nazi soldiers in every train station along the way. Maybe they won't notice me. I wish I was home with Mama and Papa.

Age 9—July 1943, Le Chambon-sur-Lignon, France

Faïdoli is the name of the house where I'm staying. All the other kids are older than me, and I think I'm the only Jew here. I'm afraid to talk to anybody. I have to always be on my guard.

There's a nice lady who works here. I think she's Jewish, but I'm not sure, and I don't dare ask. I wish I could be friends with her.

Every morning, we all have to gather in front of the house while they raise the two flags: the French flag and the Swiss one. I feel like I'm in the Scouts, or

The Swiss Aid children's home, Faïdoli

even in the army, and I don't know the rules. Everything is done a certain way. What if I make a mistake? I'm scared of the director.

IT'S BEEN A LONG TIME since I've seen such big slices of bread! Saturday night is "slices of bread" night—instead of soup, we have lots of bread, with jam and sometimes butter! I eat bread until I'm stuffed. There's also coffee with lots of milk in it, and even chocolate!

WHAT SHOULD I DO? The director said tomorrow everyone will go to services, either at the church or the Protestant temple. He's asking each of us whether we are Catholic or Protestant. Mama and Papa told me not to say I'm Jewish to anyone. But I've never heard of a Protestant and I don't know anything about being a Catholic. What will I say when he gets to me?

I TOLD THE DIRECTOR I was Catholic. Now I'm sitting in the church, waiting for my turn for confession. I have no idea what confession is and what I'm supposed to do. I'm terrified I'll do something wrong and then they'll know I'm Jewish. Maybe if I let the other kids go ahead of me, I can sneak over to the group that has already finished.

AFTER ALMOST A WEEK, I finally told the director that I had made a mistake, that I was really Protestant, not Catholic. So now I am sitting in the Protestant temple for the service. This is easier because I don't have to do anything and no one asks me anything. I can just sit here until the service is over.

It's hard to be Jewish. It's the wrong religion to be.

THERE'S LOTS TO DO HERE. We go on hikes in the woods and pick mushrooms and berries, but we don't eat the mushrooms. The director has taught us some Swiss songs and we all sing together. We're learning Scout things, like tying knots and wilderness survival. We play ball games and annoy the girls. Sometimes it's fun here, but the fear is always there in the pit of my stomach. I have to be careful of everything I say and do. I feel so alone all the time.

Age 9—August 1943, en route to Grenoble, France

I'm on my way back to Mama and Papa. The school vacation is over and Swiss Aid for Children is sending me back. They didn't send me to Switzerland. I thought they were going to save me, but they didn't. I wanted so much to tell the director that I should go, but I couldn't. I was afraid. Why didn't they want to save me?

They put me on a train all by myself. I had to change trains in Lyon. I don't even know how I did it. The station was full of Nazi soldiers. I've never been so scared in my life.

Age 9—August 1943, Grenoble, France

It's the middle of the night. The train station is almost empty. Where are Mama and Papa?

THE RED CROSS LADY at the station told me there's a curfew. She said Mama and Papa will come for me in the morning. I'm staying at her house overnight. I can't sleep. What if Mama and Papa are arrested? What if they don't come?

Age 9—October 1943, Meylan, France

Even though I didn't get to go to Switzerland, at least I'm back with Mama and Papa. Papa and I have spent a lot of time fishing pieces of wood out of the river. The wood is drying, and we'll burn it for heat this winter.

I'm back in school now. It's a country school, and most of the kids live on farms. We're learning all about farming.

Age 9—Spring 1944, Meylan, France

This morning, Nazi soldiers came and searched everywhere, even here in the school. Then we heard gunshots out back. We found out that they killed a whole Jewish family that had been hiding behind the school. Later, someone said that the postman had betrayed them. When they tried to escape, the soldiers shot them all. I'm so frightened, I feel sick. That could have been Mama and Papa and me.

EPILOGUE

American soldiers arrived in Meylan in August of 1944, when Henri Morsel was ten years old. He has a vivid memory of the first American soldier he saw—an African American named Brown, who gave him some white bread to eat.

After the war, Henri's family settled in nearby Grenoble. Henri, his mother and father, and an aunt were the only members of his family to survive the war. Henri's parents had emigrated from Poland to France three years before he was born. Their Polish accents placed them in grave danger of discovery and deportation during the war. All of Henri's other relatives had remained in Poland, and perished there.

When he was fifteen, Henri lived on a kibbutz in Israel for four months. Then he returned to France and finished high school.

His father died when Henri was only nineteen. For several years, Henri ran his father's watch business, but his mother encouraged him to go to a university. When he graduated he worked as a schoolteacher, a research scholar, and a university professor of economic history. He is now retired.

Henri is married to an English teacher, and they have two daughters. They live in Grenoble, France.

Henri did not have an easy time overcoming the constant fear he experienced during the war years. For a long time he had dreams of being in a bunker and shooting everyone who entered. His wife says, "For many years, my husband didn't wear slippers [at home]. He had to keep his shoes on, just in case we had to leave in a hurry!" He has a hard time trusting people even now.

Henri says, "You see, for me, war is a synonym for fear . . . . Because I was a child, the thing that stayed with me is the fear. Fear was our companion at every moment."

Young men in the maquis

CHAPTER FOURTEEN

Spies and Fighters
The Resistance and the Maquis

THERE WERE TWO KINDS of resistance on La Montagne Protestante during the war. One was the spiritual resistance of the people of the plateau, disobeying anti-Semitic laws that went against their beliefs. The other was the activity of the Resistance and the *maquis*.

The Resistance was made up of men and women of all religions, including Jewish refugees. Some were as young as sixteen years old. The Resistance used undercover methods to defy and disrupt the Nazis. They received secret parachute drops from England and North Africa of weapons and other important supplies. Other than robbing *gendarmeries*—police stations—this was the only way they could get guns and ammunition. The Resistance sabotaged railway lines and bombed bridges to cripple the Nazi transport system. They executed collaborators who had caused

Members of the maquis in the French Alps inspect their handiwork—
a wrecked German supply train.

others to be arrested or deported. They spread information and they spread disinformation. They also tried to convince Russian soldiers who had been forced to fight for the Nazis to switch sides. All of this was very dangerous work, because the Gestapo—Nazi secret police—was always looking for them. Across France, many men and women in the Resistance were captured and executed.

Many Resistance fighters lived double lives. Their normal daily life continued while they secretly worked to undermine the Nazis. Often, members of the Resistance were unaware of the identity of other Resistance fighters, even though they lived in the same village. It was important to keep their involvement secret.

Some of the same people who were risking their lives sheltering refugees were also doing the dangerous work of the Resistance. All the pastors of the plateau, except the pacifists Trocmé, Theis, and perhaps Bettex, were involved in the Resistance as well. The Resistance group in Le Chambon was headed by a local man named Léon Eyraud, who went by the code name "Noël."

In southern France, especially in mountainous regions, there were groups of renegade Resistance fighters. They were called the maquis. They lived rough, up in the hills. Many were fugitives from forced labor—the Nazis sent young Frenchmen to Germany to work for the Nazi empire. There were many groups of maquis on the plateau. Pierre Fayol, with his wife Marianne, French Jewish refugees, helped to organize the maquis in the Haute-Loire district of France, the district that included La Montagne Protestante. Pierre became a maquis leader, fighting with them to liberate the entire region.

Maquis and FFI fighters ride through Le Chambon after the village is liberated. The FFI—Free French Insurgency—was a very important Resistance group. It was commanded by General Charles de Gaulle, who was also the leader of the Free French government in exile in London.

Pastor Theis, who ran the Ecole Nouvelle Cévenole, had a rule: The school or the maquis, but not both of them at once! The teachers who chose to join the maquis had to quit their teaching jobs.

An American woman, Virginia Hall, had been sent to France by Allied secret services to work with the Resistance against the Nazis. She worked undercover on the plateau and was a liaison between the Allies and the maquis. She was known by two other names: Diane and La Madone—Madonna. Hall had two different disguises: as a journalist and as a peasant woman tending her flock of goats. Because of a hunting accident years earlier, she had a wooden leg, which she named Cuthbert! The Gestapo tried in vain to catch her. In fact, she was on their most-wanted list. They called her "The Limping Lady." After D-Day, in the summer of 1944, the Allies parachuted several young English officers onto the plateau to work with Virginia Hall and the Resistance, fighting the Nazis.

A photo of Peter taken in Le Chambon, for use on his false identity card

CHAPTER FIFTEEN

Sabotaging the Nazis
Peter

PETER WAS BORN IN BERLIN, *Germany, on March 1, 1929. His family moved to Austria when he was very young, and he was nine years old when the Nazis took over Austria. He came to Le Chambon when he was thirteen, and he was sixteen in 1945, when the Allies achieved victory in Europe. He told us his story at his home in Palm City, Florida, when we interviewed him on May 4, 2003.*

Age 8—1937, Vienna, Austria

Today I got baptized as a Catholic. Even though I was born Jewish, and my parents are both Jewish, I don't know anything about Judaism. We celebrate Christmas like everyone else, and the only religious education I've ever had has been Catholic. Papa says that the Nazis are only against the religious Jews and the foreign Jews, not us, but he says it's safer for me to be a real Catholic, anyway.

Age 9—March 12, 1938, Vienna, Austria

There must be thousands of people here. Hitler is speaking to the crowd from the balcony of city hall. Everyone is yelling, "*Ein Volk, Ein Reich, Ein Führer!*"— "One People, One Nation, One Leader!" I'm yelling, too.

The parade was so exciting. I'm glad I snuck away to see it. All those uniforms and the marching band. The Hitler Youth get to wear a dagger and a uniform and a black Sam Browne belt and armband, and they get to march in parades. Boy Scout uniforms aren't nearly as good as theirs, and Boy Scouts don't get daggers.

Hitler Youth in their uniforms at a Nazi rally. Their belt buckles have the words *Blut und Ehre*—"Blood and Honor"—imprinted on them.

MUTTI [MOM] IS FURIOUS. She yelled at me as soon as I walked in the door. She says a nine-year-old boy has no business running around on his own, especially now that the Nazis have taken over.

Age 9—April 1938, Brussels, Belgium

We had to leave Vienna in a hurry. I'm not sure why. All we had with us were our suitcases. We had to pretend we were just going on vacation, but really we're staying. Papa works in Antwerp, where his company has an office, and the three of us are living here in Brussels. I'm in a French-speaking school and I'm learning French as fast as I can. It's not that hard.

The first thing my parents did, as soon as we got here, was to go to the German Embassy to get new passports. Austrian passports aren't good anymore—since Germany took over, there is no more Austria. Now we have German passports.

Age 11—May 14, 1940, Brussels, Belgium

Papa thought we'd be safe here because Belgium is a neutral country. But the Nazis invaded Belgium four days ago, and now Papa has been arrested and we don't know where they're taking him. He decided to go to work just to pay his employees, in case they wanted to flee to safety. The Belgian police arrested him at the train station. Since he has a German passport now, they thought he was a German spy! Rumors are flying around that the Germans parachuted in a lot of spies before they invaded. The spies are called the fifth column. Now they think Papa is one of them. Mutti has been in a real panic. I'm worried, too.

Mutti says we have to leave Brussels. Alala, my grandmother, has been living near us. The three of us are going to take whatever we can carry and head toward France.

Age 11—May 1940, the Belgium/France border

So many people! Walking south, riding on horse-drawn carts, pushing baby carriages, trying to get to France any way they can. The roads are so crowded. Mutti has managed to get us a ride on a truck for a while. It's an ancient truck with old-fashioned tires. It's a bumpy ride, but I'm really tired of walking. I had to carry Alala's things, too. She has to walk with a cane and can't carry anything.

German airplanes keep flying over us, shooting their machine guns. I've seen people dying. They even hit some cows in the fields. I think they are trying to shoot the French and Belgian soldiers heading north to fight the Germans. But we're in the way.

The airplanes make me think of the movie I saw in Brussels, *Test Pilot*. In the movie, Clark Gable plays the pilot and he wears a white scarf and gets to fly an airplane. When I grow up, I want to be like Clark Gable and fly an airplane and go *rat-a-tat-tat* with my machine gun.

A German soldier on a motorcycle watches as people in France flee the Nazi advance.

Age 11—Summer 1940, Gurs internment camp, France

We got arrested, and now Mutti and Alala and I are in an internment camp called Gurs. We made it all the way to Paris, where my aunt lives. We had only been there a few hours when there was an air raid. Mutti said, "Let's get the hell out of here," and we took the next train south to Bordeaux. Mutti tried to register with the police there, because we were in France without permission and didn't have visas. But they didn't know what to do with us. Someone told Mutti that we should go to Oloron-Sainte-Marie. Mutti thought that was a good idea, since it is near the Spanish border. From there, we could go on to Spain if we had to.

We took the train to Oloron, but when we got there, the train was surrounded by police with machine guns. They brought us here to Gurs.

This place is horrible. They hardly give us anything to eat. We live in barracks with lots of other people. Instead of beds, we have to sleep on the floor on dirty straw. We don't even have bathrooms. The toilets are a hundred yards away from the barracks, and you have to slog through ankle-deep mud to get there. The toilets are a wooden pole across an open pit, and it stinks! A lot of people are getting sick here, and some old people have died.

Mutti is a barracks chief. She's trying to get extra food for all of us. She got some sardines from the nuns in charge of giving out food. I hate the oily taste of sardines. It reminds me of cod-liver oil.

Age 11—Autumn 1940, Auch, France

I'm so glad we got out of Gurs! One day, some Nazis came to inspect the camp, and Mutti walked right up to them and said, "*Heil* Hitler! I am a German citizen. I demand to be released from this stinking hole immediately." The Nazi officer looked at her identity papers and saw that she had a German passport. He couldn't tell that she was Jewish, because the passport didn't have a *J* stamped on it. When Mutti got her new passport in Belgium, they weren't doing that yet. Now, if you're Jewish, they mark it on your passport with a big *J*. The Nazi officer turned to the camp commander and told him to call a taxi, pay the driver, and take us wherever we want to go.

The cabdriver told us there was no way to get across the Spanish border, so Mutti and Alala and I headed north in the taxi. When we got to Auch, the people told us, "Don't go any farther. The Germans are on the other side of town." So we stopped here.

We stayed in a convent for a few weeks. Alala was able to join my aunt in the United States, so she left. Now it's just Mutti and me. We have a one-room apartment. Mutti is working for a refugee relief organization run by Quakers and Swiss Aid for Children, and she's trying to find out where Papa is.

Age 12—1941, Auch, France

Papa is back! Mutti finally found out that he was in a French internment camp called St. Cyprien, right on the Mediterranean Sea. He said that they had to live in tents right on the sand, and it was boiling hot in the summer and freezing cold in the winter. He had gotten so sick that they thought he was going to die, so they gave him a thirty-day sick leave to come home. Little by little, he's getting better, but he's still weak. Every month, Mutti gets his thirty-day leave renewed, but we're never sure if they'll send him back to the camps. He's not allowed to work, but he's started a small business, anyway, cleaning used spark plugs. You can't get new ones anymore, because of the war. He's applied for visas for us to go to America.

I'm in the Boy Scouts here, and last summer I got to go to summer camp. I'm really glad Papa is here with us.

Age 13—Spring 1942, Auch, France

Last winter, Papa succeeded in getting us all visas, but only the ones for me and Mutti arrived. Mutti refused to leave without him. His visa just arrived last week, but ours have expired now. He won't go without us. We're trying to get ours renewed.

Age 13—August 27, 1942, Condom, France

I can't stop thinking about my parents. I got really bad news today. Mutti and Papa have been arrested. Madame Cavailhon, the director of my summer camp, called me to her office and told me.

I remember my parents whispering, right before I left for camp, that the Germans and the *gendarmes*—police—were rounding up Jews, that it was getting dangerous. They thought I didn't hear them, but I did. They whispered that people were being shipped east to Poland. Now they've been arrested. I'm not sure what this means, but I'm so frightened for them. I can't stop crying.

A couple of weeks ago, Papa came to visit me here. He brought me a small bag that my mother had made out of a handkerchief and told me to keep it. After Papa left, I thought about him bicycling twenty miles here and twenty miles back. Why would he make all that effort when he is still so sick? I looked in the bag. It had Mutti's jewelry and Papa's gold pocket watch in it. Suddenly I thought, This is the last time that I will ever see Papa. And I started crying.

Now I am all alone. I've started a diary. I'm writing it to my parents. It makes me feel like I'm talking to them when I write in it, and this way they will know what I'm doing in their absence. Madame Cavailhon said that we're going to say a novena—nine days of prayers with a rosary—and when we're finished, Mutti and Papa will come back.

Age 13—August 29, 1942, Condom, France

I got a card from my parents today. They say that they are together and have been taken to a camp called Le Vernet. I hope that soon they will be released. I am writing in my diary every day.

Age 13—September 1, 1942, Condom, France

At lunch, Madame Cavailhon ordered me to go to bed. She said that she had been warned that the gendarmes would be coming this afternoon to arrest me. The person who warned her said that if I was sick, they wouldn't arrest me. So she said that I should have a high fever. She made balls out of bread and soaked them in vinegar, and then she told me to swallow them whole. I had to swallow ten of them, one after another. It made me break out in a fever. When the gendarmes came, they didn't take me away.

Age 13—September 5, 1942, Condom, France

It's been nine days. The novena is finished. But my parents haven't come back.

Age 13—September 28, 1942, Condom, France

Madame Cavailhon sent me to bed during dinner. The gendarmes came for me again. That makes three times they've come to arrest me, and every time I've had a fever. This time, they said that within forty-eight hours we have to show them a medical certificate saying that I'm too ill to be moved, or they will arrest me, anyway. I'm scared. And they didn't even care that I had gotten a telegram from the Vichy government saying that I have permission to leave France. I'm supposed to go on a children's transport ship organized by Quakers, and go to America.

Mutti and Papa are in a camp called Drancy, near Paris. I'm so worried. I hadn't heard from them for thirteen days, when I got their second postcard. I cry a lot thinking of them. I know I shouldn't get discouraged. I should be brave and wait. But I am so afraid for them.

Age 13—October 12, 1942, Condom, France

Madame Cavailhon sent me to talk to the archbishop today. She said she couldn't answer all my questions. I have been angry ever since we said the novena for my parents and it didn't work. The archbishop told me that there are no answers to my questions. He said that is what is called faith. I don't think I have faith anymore.

Age 13—October 17, 1942, Condom, France

Nothing new. Thinking of my parents.

Age 13—January 1943, Marseille, France

I've been in three different children's homes in Marseille since I got here last November, and now they want to send me someplace else. Madame Cavailhon brought me to Marseille to take the Quaker ship to America. But right before it was supposed to sail the Germans took over the southern part of France, and no more ships could leave Marseille. So I'm stuck here.

I got in a lot of trouble for talking to some German SS soldiers. They were staying across the street, and I just started talking to them one day. After all, I speak German. They were very friendly. They gave me chocolate and invited me to their spaghetti dinners. It was great. But when the director of that children's home found out, he said I was endangering everybody else, and he sent me here. I hate this new place. Now they are going to send me someplace up in the mountains to live. It's called Le Chambon.

Age 13—January 17, 1943, Le Chambon-sur-Lignon, France

I was up really late last night. I had to take the first streetcar at 6:00 in the morning yesterday to get to the Marseille train station, and my train didn't get into St. Agrève until 11:49 last night. Monsieur Daniel Trocmé had come on his bicycle to meet me. All I had was my backpack. We had to walk fifteen kilometers through the snow to get to Les Grillons, the children's home where I'm staying. It was bitter cold. We didn't talk much while we were walking, but Monsieur Trocmé seemed very nice. He's the director of Les Grillons. As soon as we got here, I had something warm to eat and then fell right asleep.

It's very clean here. I think I'm going to like it. Little by little, I'm meeting the other kids. Amédée is here. I know him from the summer camp in Condom. He came here last September.

Age 14—May 1943, Le Chambon-sur-Lignon, France

I've fallen in love! Her name is Rosario. She's a refugee from the Spanish Civil War, and she's beautiful. I think she's a couple of years older than me, maybe sixteen, but she likes me, too. There are about twenty-five of us living in Les Grillons. About half are Jewish. We come from Austria, Czechoslovakia, Belgium, all over. There's even a German army deserter here. Most of the kids don't like him, but I think he's okay.

I'm going to school here, at the Ecole Nouvelle Cévenole. It takes about an

Peter doing schoolwork at Les Grillons. He is fourth from the left, smiling at the camera. [Chambon Foundation]

Children from Les Grillons pull a cart, laden with supplies, through the snow.

hour to walk into the village from Les Grillons. Then we have to go all over the place for our different classes. After school, we take turns bringing food back on a cart for everyone. The cart has two bicycle wheels, and we have to push and pull it up the steep hill to Les Grillons. That's much easier now that the snow has melted. We also take turns helping in the kitchen, peeling potatoes and chopping vegetables.

Several times, they've told us to drop what we're doing and go look for mushrooms in the woods. I don't understand that. We're not going to find mushrooms in May. September is mushroom season. We might find some wild blueberries soon, but no mushrooms.

I'm outgrowing my shoes, but I refuse to wear the ugly sandals Monsieur Trocmé is making for everyone. They're made out of old tires and rope. Who ever heard of sandals like that!

It's been a long time since I was able to write in my diary. Monsieur Trocmé took it away a couple of weeks after I got here. I guess he thought it was too risky, because I wrote down the names of all the people who helped me get here. I'll just have to remember everything to tell Mutti and Papa, if I ever see them again. I really miss them.

Age 14—August 1943, Le Chambon-sur-Lignon, France

My name is now Pierre Fesson, instead of Peter Feigl. My birth date is the same, but my new identity card says I was born in France. They've told me that I speak the language well enough to pass as a real French kid, and they've made me a whole set of false papers, ration cards, and everything. Everyone who is leaving has gotten them. Some of us are being sent away to boarding school somewhere else.

They took lots of photos of us to use in the false papers, and they've given us all the extras. We're all exchanging photos. I wrote on the back of the one I gave Rosario: "To my love, from her admiring Peter." She wrote on the back of mine, too: "To my funny Pierrot." I'm going to write everyone's real name and false name on the back of the photos I collect, so I will remember them.

Age 14—November 1943, Figeac, France

The kids I came here with from Le Chambon don't like me. Well, I don't like them, either. They think I'm anti-Semitic just because I made some remarks. I spend all my free time reading, anyway. And I go to the movies whenever I can.

Most of the kids in my boarding school are Catholic. In order to be safe, the rest of us have to pretend to be Catholic. That's no problem for me. Although I don't believe anymore, I decided to be an altar boy. Anyone who sees me in church will think I'm a real Catholic. The others resent me for it.

Age 14—January 1944, Figeac, France

The *maquis*—Resistance fighters—have blown up the Ratier factory here in town. Altogether, we heard eight explosions. They're trying to make things hard on the Germans.

Age 15—March 21, 1944, Figeac, France

Last night, there was an air raid.

Age 15—April 26, 1944, Figeac, France

I'm going to be expelled from school. German soldiers are all over town now. We've heard shooting, and sometimes we hear military planes overhead. A bunch of us decided to slash the tires of some German trucks. Somehow, the school director found out and now I'm in big trouble. I think they're making plans to send me away.

Age 15—Early May 1944, Figeac, France

There are German army trucks everywhere. They've even taken over the school yard. The maquis have asked me to keep my ears open. They know I understand German. Last month they asked me to translate some German papers that they had stolen. They want me to let them know what the Germans are saying. If I can find out what they're going to do next, it will really help the maquis.

Some of us here at the school have decided to pour sugar into the gas tanks of the German trucks. Everyone knows that's the best way to ruin a truck. It will run for a few minutes, and then it will freeze up.

Age 15—May 12, 1944, Figeac, France

I'm hiding. I'm as high up as I can get in the church bell tower. I don't think anyone saw me come up here. I don't want them to take me away. A German SS detachment has come to Figeac. The maquis are fighting them. Things have really heated up here. The Germans have ordered all the men between the ages of sixteen and fifty-four to report to the *gendarmerie*—police station. I'm only fifteen and a half, but I'm not going to take any chances.

Age 15—May 14, 1944, Figeac, France

The Germans finally left. I came down from the bell tower after hiding up there for twenty-four hours. They got Jean Siroit. His real name is Jean Spiegel. I know him from Le Chambon. He is three years older than me.

The maquis have heard rumors that the Germans have figured out that somebody in the school is watching them and reporting on them. I'm probably going to have to leave now. It's too dangerous for me here.

Age 15—May 22, 1944, en route to Switzerland

What's wrong with the other kids? Don't they know we have to get off the train here at Viry? This is where we're supposed to meet the *passeurs*—people smugglers—who will take us over the border into Switzerland. I can't ask them what they're doing because we have to pretend we don't know each other. They're just sitting there. Well, I'm not going to wait. We were told to get off here, and I'm getting off. The train is moving again. I'm going to have to jump off.

I FOUND THE PASSEURS. There are other people here, too, waiting to cross the border, and we all have to hide in a field. Some police go by. I don't think they can see us. When the other kids from the train get here, we start walking. We cross more fields and then go into a forest. The passeurs get lost for a while. A little kid is making too much noise and the passeurs get mad. I wish that kid would shut up.

Now we can see the border—two rows of barbed-wire fences—and the Swiss buildings beyond. But we can't cross over yet. We have to wait until the changing of the guards. The passeurs tell us to lie down in the grass. It's been raining, and now the grass is soaking wet. We wait.

We get the signal to go. We stand up, and then we see that there are other people waiting here to cross the border, too. Maybe twenty of us in all. Everyone runs toward the barbed-wire fences. I throw my backpack over the first fence, and then I cross. I'm running for the second fence, a hundred yards ahead, when a young girl yells, "We're heading the wrong way!" She turns around and starts running back. She had seen what she thought was a German soldier on the other side of the second fence. Some others turn back, too. Then, someone starts shooting and I hear screams.

She was wrong about the soldier. I don't think he's German, because German soldiers don't carry their rifles that way, cradled in their arms. The helmet

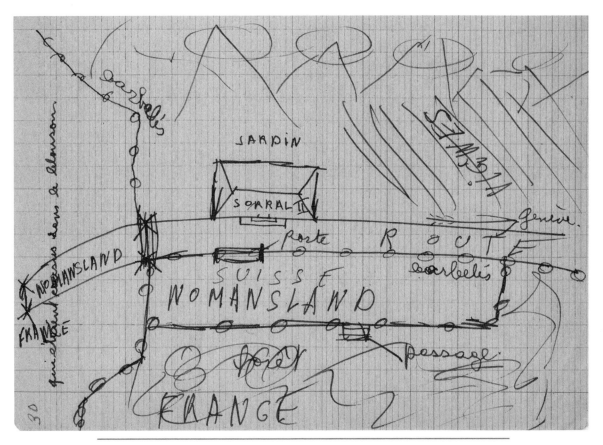

Shortly after his escape into Switzerland, Peter drew this map of his border crossing in his diary. The writing is in French: *Suisse*—Switzerland; *barbelés*—barbed-wire; *forêt*—forest; *porte*—door or gate; *jardin*—garden; *route*—road. He wrote *Sorral II* over the guardhouse. It was the name of the place on the Swiss border where he crossed over. The guard he described was standing between the barbed-wire fence and the guardhouse at Sorral II.

doesn't look right, either. I keep going straight, and I'm the first one over the barbed wire.

The soldier hasn't moved. He hasn't said a word. But now he says to me, "Get behind the buildings!" And I run. I'm in Switzerland!

Epilogue

Peter Feigl never saw his parents again. In 1950, he finally learned from the International Red Cross that they had been sent to Auschwitz and perished there. Decades later, he found out that they had been transported to Auschwitz from Drancy only days after being arrested.

His grandmother and an aunt, who had come to the United States from France during the war, sponsored him to immigrate. He came to the United States from Switzerland in July 1946 at the age of seventeen. He brought with him fifty-eight photographs of his friends in Le Chambon.

He worked briefly in New York City, then spent three years in the air force. After a number of years working in the international operations of aviation companies, and traveling all over the world, he went to work for the Pentagon, rising to the position of Deputy for Management to the Deputy Assistant Secretary of Defense for International Security Affairs.

He married another German refugee. They have two children and two grandchildren. He and his wife now live in Florida.

In the 1980s, forty years after his diary was taken away in Le Chambon, he learned that it had been published in France. The publisher had found the diary in a flea market in southern France. The publisher assumed that the author of the diary had died in the war, but then saw him in Weapons of the Spirit, *a documentary film about Le Chambon, and contacted him. The diary is now in the collection of the United States Holocaust*

Memorial Museum in Washington, D.C., along with the photos he brought from Le Chambon.

He says, "I've been teaching in some of the schools here. . . . They call me . . . when they teach them about the Holocaust. . . . My message is that I stand before you because some people decided to do what's right instead of what's convenient, or what's safe. Some people stuck their necks out. If it hadn't been for someone in the gendarmerie to warn, if it hadn't been for the people at the children's home at the time my parents were arrested to make the arrangements to get me out, if it hadn't been for the people of Le Chambon, I wouldn't be here."

Jean is out for a walk near Le Chambon in 1942. With him are Mademoiselle Usach, director of La Guespy, and Jean's sister, Anne-Marie. You can see Mont Lizieux off in the distance behind them.

CHAPTER SIXTEEN

In the Maquis
Jean

ALTHOUGH HE WAS NOT *a Jewish refugee, Jean came to Le Chambon as an orphan in need of shelter. We interviewed him at his home in Paris, France, on November 14, 2002.*

LA MONTAGNE PROTESTANTE took in many people in need during the war. Not all of them were Jewish refugees. Jean and his sister, Anne-Marie, came to Le Chambon in 1941 from another part of France. Their parents had both passed away, and now Jean and Anne-Marie were orphans. They had nowhere to go. Jean's classics teacher was a Protestant who knew about Le Chambon, and he helped them to go there.

Jean was sixteen years old when he arrived in Le Chambon, and his sister was fourteen. They lived at La Guespy, one of the Swiss Aid homes, for three years. It

La Guespy in 1941 or 1942. Jean is standing on the bottom left windowsill.

was there that Jean first understood what the Vichy laws against Jews really meant. He had been raised agnostic, and his family had been country folk. They hadn't come into contact with anyone Jewish. In Le Chambon, Jean lived with many Jewish teenagers, and he went to school with them as well. He even celebrated Hanukkah with them at La Guespy. This was the first time he had ever gotten to know any Jews. The anti-Semitic laws in France became real to him.

Life at La Guespy was busy with chores and games. Each evening, they all sat around one big table to do their homework. In summer, they went hiking and swam in the Lignon River. One day, when they were swimming, a man started to drown.

They all went to help, and pulled him out. Luis, a young Spanish refugee, resuscitated him, using Jean's back to prop him up. Then they realized that the man was a German soldier, one of those who were convalescing from war wounds at the Hotel du Lignon in the village. Later, there was a tragic raid at La Maison des Roches, where Luis was living, and he was arrested. When they learned that he had helped to save the drowning soldier, the Gestapo—Nazi secret police—released him.

Winter was harsh, and there was no hot water for taking baths at La Guespy. It was cold out and the snow was deep, but most of the time, the boys wore shorts. Everybody wore *sabots*—wooden clogs.

Food was precious. Although the young people at La Guespy were fed well, especially compared with children in the cities in France, it still didn't feel like quite enough to a growing teenage boy. When they went out on walks, they would dig up carrots from the fields and eat them as they walked along. Mademoiselle Usach, the director of the home, kept the chocolate, cheese, and halvah that came from Switzerland hidden up in the attic, to be doled out a little at a time.

Students at the Ecole Nouvelle Cévenole studied hard. The teachers expected the students to be honest and disciplined—they didn't even supervise them during exams. At the Ecole Nouvelle Cévenole, it was the first time Jean had been in a classroom with both boys and girls.

At school, they would get the latest radio reports from London. Jean's Greek teacher was married to a man in the *maquis*—Resistance fighters. Jean knew what was going on, and he knew about the maquis. One day, someone contacted him about joining. He explained to Jean that he was organizing groups of six people each, and that they would be supervised by maquis leader Pierre Fayol. Each group would be separate, not knowing what the others were doing, or even who they were. This way, no one could betray any other groups if they were caught. Jean didn't want to endanger the others at La Guespy, so when he joined the maquis he moved out.

Jean was in a group with Virginia Hall. She knew all the radio codes. She was the person who communicated with Allied secret services, coordinating parachute

One of the fifteen parachute drops that took place just outside of Villelonge, a village about two and a half miles south of Le Chambon. [Chambon Foundation]

drops from England or Algiers of food, ammunition, or even people. Sometimes the parachutes would bring maple syrup and American cigarettes!

The parachute drops were made at night. A coded message, such as "A robin sings in the morning," would let them know where and when the drop would take place. On the appointed night, members of the maquis would mark the perimeter of the field with small lights so that the pilot would know exactly where to make the drop. Jean would hear the plane approaching, then he'd hear the pilot speaking in English over the radio transmitter to Hall. She would give the proper coded response, so the pilot would know that it was safe. Then the plane would circle, make the drop, and fly away. As soon as the parachute had landed, Jean and the others would hide the cargo.

As the Allies were driving the German army out of France in 1944, the Free French Army, which had been fighting in Africa, came back to France. Jean joined up, and fought the Nazis in France and Germany. He left the army after the war was over in 1945, and went to live in Paris with the Meyer family (*see* Chapter Seventeen, "A Bright Spirit: Lise"). His close friend Francis, their son, had been killed in battle. The Meyers treated him like part of the family. They sent him to medical school, and he went on to become a doctor. Today, Jean Nallet and his wife live in Paris. He's still in touch with friends that he made in Le Chambon.

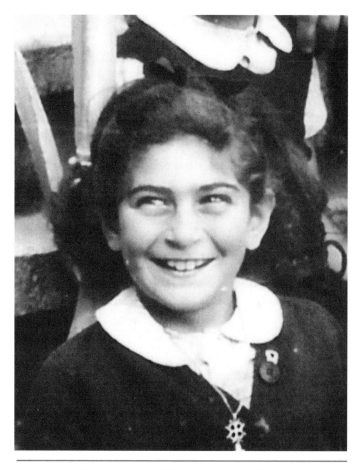

Lise in Le Chambon, 1943, with her irresistable smile

CHAPTER SEVENTEEN

A Bright Spirit
Lise

LISE WAS BORN IN PARIS, *France, on December 6, 1933. She was six years old when the Nazis invaded France. She came to Le Chambon when she was eight, and she was eleven when the Allies achieved victory in Europe. She gave us permission to tell her story based on an unpublished memoir she had written for her grandchildren.*

LISE-HÉLÈNE CAME FROM A happy family, and the four children were very close. The two older brothers were protective of their younger sisters, even though they teased their sisters mercilessly. Bernard, the oldest, took special care of Ariane, while Francis felt very protective of Lise, the baby of the family.

Lise was six when France fell to the Nazis. From that point on, everything began to change. Her father, a successful doctor, was forced to give up his work, because Jews were forbidden to practice medicine. Everyone in Lise's family had to wear a yellow star whenever they went out, to signify that they were Jewish.

Life in Paris became difficult. They no longer had heat in their building. During the winter, they turned on a small space heater in their apartment just during meals and baths, and for a little while right before bedtime. It was so cold at night that Lise and her sister and brothers wore sweaters over their pajamas, thick socks, and sometimes even woolen caps to bed.

There was very little to eat. Lise and her family couldn't be choosy—they ate whatever they were able to get. Often, her mother would have to wake up very early to go stand in line for hours at the store, just to get some potatoes and a little milk and sugar. Sometimes the children would take her place in line, so that she could have a break.

During the first two years of the Nazi occupation, Lise's saddest memory was of her brothers leaving Paris. Teenage Jewish boys were in danger of being arrested. Their parents felt that the boys would be safer in the Unoccupied Southern Zone. An aunt lived in Lyon, so that's where Bernard and Francis went.

Early one morning in June 1942, Lise's parents gently woke the girls, telling them to get dressed—the family was leaving Paris. Their parents had known for several weeks that they were going. They had made all the arrangements but had said nothing to the girls. They hadn't wanted to frighten them, and they were concerned that the girls might give away their plans by saying good-bye to their friends. Within an hour, they left for the train station, Lise's father carrying only one suitcase for all of them.

They were headed south. They planned to meet a *passeur*—people smuggler—who would take them across the demarcation line between Occupied France and the Southern Zone. The express trains were closely watched by German soldiers. Lise's family took the local trains instead, making many stops, changing trains often, and crawling along at a very slow pace. Lise and her sister, Ariane, had to pretend they didn't know their father. This was a precaution—if he were arrested, perhaps the girls would have a chance of escaping, if no one knew they were with him.

When they reached the town of Moulin, they met with the passeur. He was upset. He told them that six others, who were supposed to cross the border with them, had stopped for something to eat. Afterward, those people had flagged down a truck for a ride, but it was full of German soldiers and they were all arrested. He told them that the soldiers were looking for them, and the soldiers had dogs. There was no possibility of their crossing over into southern France until the German soldiers were gone. They would have to hide.

He led them deep into the woods, where Lise and her family all crowded together in a ditch. He gave them some bread and cheese, and they waited, listening for every little sound.

In the middle of the night, the passeur returned. He led them through the dark woods for hours. The girls were terrified. Ariane walked holding her mother's hand, while the passeur hoisted little Lise up onto his shoulders for a time.

Finally, the passeur stopped. He told them all to hold hands and crawl through a thicket of underbrush. On the other side they were to run, one at a time, as fast as they could for another twenty yards. They followed his directions. The passeur joined them there, and said, "You've made it. You're in the Southern Zone."

He brought them to a small, run-down hotel. Lise and her family collapsed on the bed, and all four of them slept until noon the next day.

When the family arrived in Lyon, Lise got to see her beloved brothers. But Lyon wasn't their final destination. They were headed for Le Chambon-sur-Lignon.

Once in Le Chambon, Lise's father joined the *maquis*—Resistance fighters—and eventually her brothers did, too. Her father became the head doctor for the maquis in the nearby region of Ardèche, and Lise's mother went with him. Lise was eight years old and her sister was ten. They stayed in Le Chambon, at the *pension*—boardinghouse—Tante Soly, right in the center of the village.

The two girls loved it at Tante Soly. They were very happy there. It was run by a Jewish refugee, Monsieur Sèches, who had come to Le Chambon with his family. *Oncle* [Uncle] Tom and *Tante* [Aunt] Soly were a warm and loving couple, and they

A group picture at Tante Soly. Emile Sèches—Oncle Tom—is holding a little girl. Lise is standing in the second row, all the way to the right. [Chambon Foundation]

took care of not only their own three young children but also fifteen others, most of them Jewish.

All of the children from Tante Soly went to school in the village. In the evenings, they did their homework together under the watchful eye of Oncle Tom. On Saturdays, they went to the movies at Le Chambon's only movie theater, where they met with many of the kids from the other pensions.

Winter lasted five months on the plateau, and Lise and her friends enjoyed all the snow. One of their favorite things to do was to go sledding. Sometimes, they would make a train of sleds. They would lie on their stomachs on their sleds, often with another kid piled on top. Then they'd each hook their feet onto the sled behind them, and the whole train of sleds would go speeding through the village, from the town hall all the way down to the river. If they were caught, they'd get in trouble. They weren't supposed to sled down the streets!

The children also skiied, but they didn't have fancy equipment. Lise called her skis "old planks of wood." Nobody had ski boots, and it was difficult to ski in *sabots*—wooden clogs. The cobbler drilled a slot through the heels of their wooden clogs. That way, the children could thread the straps through to hold on their skis.

One day, Lise and her friend Philippe Sèches set off on skis to a farm several miles away, to get some milk, butter, and cheese for the household. The children often went to the neighboring farms to get food for the pension. When Lise and Philippe returned to Tante Soly, they were freezing. Lise was in a rush to get inside so she could warm up. She bent over to take off her skis without first removing her knapsack. Unfortunately, that was where the container of milk was—and the top had not been securely fastened. As she bent over, all five liters of milk spilled out. She was drenched! Philippe thought it was very funny.

Lise's mother returned to Le Chambon for several months, and the girls lived with her in a small apartment. Lise's father and brothers visited when they could. Later, the girls returned to Tante Soly.

Lise liked school, but she often got in trouble for laughing and joking with her classmates. One day, her teacher met with Lise's mother to discuss Lise's frequent disruptions of class. Her mother suggested that Lise be moved to another part of the room. The teacher said that it didn't matter where Lise sat. She would always be the center of the laughter and jokes!

Lise's teacher often tried to punish her, but it backfired every time. Lise was thrilled to be sent out of class. She would just go visit her mother. When she was caught making mischief with some other kids, the teacher

Young skiers having fun on the plateau

would send the troublemakers to chop firewood for her. But they thought it was much more fun to chop firewood together than to have to sit in class.

Despite all the pranks and fun, Lise was an excellent student. When she graduated to middle school, she became more serious about her studies. Her teachers inspired her, and she decided that she wanted to become a teacher, too.

The years she spent in Le Chambon passed happily for Lise. When she was ten years old, Le Chambon and the surrounding area were liberated. She has vivid memories of French flags appearing in all the windows and tanks rolling through the village. All the children tried to climb up on the tanks, so that they could hug the soldiers and beg for chewing gum and chocolate!

Fighting continued elsewhere in France and in Germany. Lise's family remained

Le Chambon, 1942. Lise (on right), the youngest in her family, with her sister and brothers, (from left) Bernard, Ariane, and Francis.

French flags fly from the windows and people wave as French soldiers roll through Le Chambon on September 3, 1944.

on La Montagne Protestante for almost another year. On the seventh of May 1945, the war ended in Europe. There was singing and dancing in the streets, with kids dancing along in snaking lines throughout the village. Everybody celebrated.

The following autumn, Lise's family finally went home—all of them but Francis. He had been killed fighting the Germans in Alsace.

Epilogue

It was not easy for Lise-Hélène Meyer and her sister to adjust to life back in Paris. After three years in the country, the city seemed loud, dangerous, busy, and polluted. For a time, they were afraid even to go out by themselves. Kind friends, who had stayed in Paris throughout the occupation, would accompany them out, until they got used to the city once more.

The Meyers were back in their own apartment, and gradually their old life resumed. Lise's father started up his practice again, and her mother found many of her old friends. Bernard married his sweetheart, and the girls went back to school.

But there was a hole in their lives where Francis had been. They had a letter he had written to them just before he was killed. In the letter, he said that if he were to die in the war, he had a request: that his parents do something to help his good friend Jean Nallet (see Chapter Sixteen, "In the Maquis: Jean"). Jean wanted to become a doctor, but he was an orphan, with a sister to support, and he could not afford to go to medical school. The Meyers invited Jean to live with them in Paris, and they offered to send him to medical school. Jean accepted their offer and became like a big brother to Lise and Ariane.

When she grew up, Lise Meyer Martinon got married and fulfilled her dream of becoming a teacher. For many years, she taught French, Latin, and Greek, and now she is retired. She lives in a suburb of Paris, and she has seven grandchildren.

The pension Beau Soleil was on this street in Le Chambon called the route de Tence. It was located not far behind the person who took this photograph.

CHAPTER EIGHTEEN

House of Refuge and Resistance

Gabrielle

GABRIELLE GREW UP IN LE CHAMBON. *We interviewed her at her home there on April 6, 2004.*

GABRIELLE TURNED EIGHTEEN IN 1940, the year the Nazis occupied France. Almost everyone in her family was involved in resisting the Nazis and the Vichy regime. Her mother ran the Beau Soleil *pension*—boardinghouse—in Le Chambon and took in many Jewish refugees, whether they could pay or not. One day, Gaby's father said that they might as well just hang a sign out front saying they were running a charity!

Gaby's family didn't get advance warning. Refugees would just show up, and her mother would make room for them. Often, the family would help find places on the plateau that were more isolated, where refugees could hide. It was too dangerous for some of them to stay at Beau Soleil, right in the village.

Gaby's father was in the Resistance and worked with the *maquis*—Resistance fighters—along with Léon Eyraud, the leader of Le Chambon's Resistance.

Both her mother and her father needed false papers. Her father needed false papers for the maquis, and her mother needed false ration cards so she could feed all the Jewish refugees staying at Beau Soleil. They both turned to Gaby to make them. During the war, she made false papers for anyone who asked, whenever she could.

Gaby used the same process of making false papers as a number of others, including another local, Sammy Charles, and a Jewish refugee named Oscar Rosowsky, who had stayed at Beau Soleil for a while when he first came to Le Chambon. Gaby would trace the stamp from an authentic identity card and transfer it to a false card, using a gelatin-covered strip of cloth heated over a candle. It was tricky, because the gelatin would drip off if she heated it too much. If she didn't heat it enough, the transfer wouldn't work. She could get four or five prints from each gelatin transfer, then she had to start over with a new tracing.

Because Gaby was away at school, she could only work on the false papers on holidays and during the summer, when she was home. There was no privacy at school, and she had nowhere to hide all her materials.

During her last year of school she moved to a nearby village, where she had her own apartment. She began making false papers there as well. Her younger brother and sister would ride over from Le Chambon on their bicycles to give her the materials and information she needed. When the false papers were completed, she would mail them back to Le Chambon to be delivered. False papers for the refugees might go to Magda Trocmé or to Gaby's mother at Beau Soleil. Papers for the maquis would go to her father or to Monsieur Eyraud. Later, Gaby would recognize people on the street from the photographs on the false papers she had made for them. She would think to herself, Aha! I know about you!

It was very dangerous work. She would certainly have been arrested if she had been caught. She remembers being afraid only once. One day, she was taking the train back from Le Chambon. When she entered the train compartment, she saw that the only other person in it was a German soldier. It was too late for her to turn around and leave. She was terrified that he would find out what was in her suitcase and arrest her. Her suitcase was full of all the materials she needed to make more false papers! He politely took the suitcase from her and placed it in the luggage net above. Then they both sat down. What a nerve-racking ride back it must have been!

In addition to making false papers, Gaby risked her life helping to lead Jewish refugees toward Switzerland. Many refugees were guided to Switzerland by bus and train. But others, whose appearances were considered by the Nazis to look Jewish, couldn't travel openly. Even false identity cards wouldn't help them. So they were led by more clandestine routes, on foot through the woods, where no one would see them. Gaby guided these refugees from Le Chambon on the first part of their journey to Switzerland.

She would lead a small group of Jewish refugees through the woods all day. That night, the refugees would sleep in a pastor's house, while Gaby would sleep in a barn in the hay. The next morning, someone else would take over, guiding the refugees on the next stage of their journey, while Gaby would take the entire day returning to Le Chambon. The refugees would spend days getting to Switzerland, stopping overnight at pastors' houses or other safe homes or convents along the way.

In Le Chambon, Gaby helped her mother run the pension. There were a lot of mouths to feed. Students of the Ecole Nouvelle Cévenole, some of whom were refugees, stayed there, and others as well. One rabbi lived at Beau Soleil for three years. Then there were the six members of Gaby's family and their lone employee.

It wasn't easy to find enough food each day. The ration cards only allowed for meat once a week, and Gaby's mother didn't think that was enough for teenage boys. Sometimes, she sent her children to the farms on the plateau to buy a pig. Sometimes, they would buy a sheep. Gaby's sister would carry the sheep across her shoulders back to the pension.

Gaby's mother was a courageous woman who kept her head in an emergency. One day, she saw the Gestapo—Nazi secret police—right outside the window. They were heading toward the door. The boys who were staying at Beau Soleil had just sat down to eat. She ran into the dining room and warned them all to stay where they were and keep on eating. If any of them went upstairs to hide, it would look suspicious, and they would probably be arrested. She let the Gestapo in and calmly pointed out that these were just students having their lunch. Soon the Gestapo left. She had maintained her cool while the Gestapo were there, but for the rest of the day, she was rattled. She told Gaby afterward, "I made blood pudding later that day, and I don't know what happened, but the sauce was so thick that the spoon could stand straight up in it!"

One day near the end of the war, the family suffered a terrible tragedy. The maquis had been fighting to liberate the plateau, but the Germans were advancing. Many of the maquis had taken shelter in Beau Soleil. People said that the Germans were heading toward Le Chambon, and everyone was afraid. That day, Gaby's sister, Manou, was accidentally shot and killed with a gun that the maquis had left in the pension.

Rather than reacting with anger or hatred against the boy who had fired the shot, Gaby's mother kept him safe at the pension for two days, until the German advance was halted, and it was safe for him to leave.

Gaby's brave work to help save the lives of Jewish refugees was recognized when

Israel's Holocaust museum, Yad Vashem, awarded her the title "Righteous Among the Nations," in 1988. The title was awarded jointly to Gaby and her mother, Georgette Barraud, for their dedication and courage.

Gaby Barraud lives in Le Chambon, and she is still in close contact with her friends and fellow makers of false papers, Sammy Charles and Oscar Rosowsky.

LE CHAMBON-DE-TENCE (Hte-Loire) alt. 969 m. — Cure d'air - La Gare

S. Bard, éditeur

A train arrives at the station in Le Chambon.

CHAPTER NINETEEN

Hiding Children
OSE and Madeleine Dreyfus

OSE (OEUVRE DE SECOURS AUX ENFANTS) was a French Jewish organization that was committed to helping Jewish refugee children. Madeleine Dreyfus, a Jew from Paris, had been working with them as a psychologist. In the summer of 1942, she was put in charge of bringing Jewish children to La Montagne Protestante. Her first contact there was in Le Chambon, with Pastor Trocmé and his wife, Magda.

Several times a month, Madame Dreyfus would take the train from Lyon with a group of refugee children. She would warn them not to speak in any language other than French during the train ride. She would tell them what to expect when they arrived. Usually she and the children would be met at the Le Chambon train station by Madame Déléage or her daughter, Eva. Then they would drop the children off at the Hôtel May, by the station, and go off in search of farmers who would take the children in. They were discreet, never saying out loud that these were Jewish children.

The Déléage family sheltered many Jewish children in their own home in the hamlet of Les Tavas, near Le Chambon. One time, Madame Déléage had been warned that the Gestapo—Nazi secret police—were coming. She sat calmly outside her house, arms crossed, waiting for them to arrive. When they got there, they asked her where the Jewish children were. She pretended she couldn't understand what they were saying. They repeated the question again and again, until finally they left in disgust. They never did find the children, who had been sent to hide in the woods nearby.

Once when Madame Dreyfus was leaving Le Chambon by train, she overheard two *gendarmes*—policemen—talking. "We didn't find any Jews there," they said, "but we sure did eat well!" Apparently, someone in Le Chambon had succeeded in distracting the gendarmes from their mission by plying them with sausages and cheese!

Most of the farmers on the plateau were poor, and it was expensive to care for extra children. The farmers generally had enough food, but OSE gave each of them a small amount of money to help pay for things like extra soap and visits to the doctor. Madame Dreyfus came to Le Chambon twice a month to check on the children that she had hidden there. She brought clothes, medicine, and food ration cards for the children. She talked with the families and made sure that the children had everything they needed. She also brought letters to the children from their parents whenever she could. Often their parents did not even know where OSE had hidden their children—it was safer that way—and so this was the only way they could communicate with them.

The farmers generally were devoted to the children in their care. Louise and Arthur Franc took in Pierre Cohen, a Jewish boy from Belgium, when he was nine years old. He lived with them for two and a half years. Madame Franc introduced

The Francs, posing in the doorway of their farmhouse with a shepherd boy and three young Jews whom they sheltered in their home. Pierre Cohen stands directly in front of Madame Franc.

him as her son, and the Francs loved him dearly. Shortly before he was to be reunited with his mother at the end of the war, Madame Franc wrote to her, saying: "You have, dear lady, such a beautiful boy, and it is my greatest joy to take care of him. Truly, my husband and I are proud of him. To separate us, we will all need handkerchiefs." The Francs and Pierre stayed in touch after the war. Pierre said, "At eighty-five years of age, Louise still remembers all of my childhood pranks and adores reminding me of them."

Often, the children would be given chores to do, even the very youngest. They would be asked to help keep an eye on the cows or collect pinecones to use for kindling. They spent just as much time inventing games as doing these chores, but the farmers didn't seem to mind.

Life on the farms of La Montagne Protestante was very different from what many of the children had been used to. For the most part, the people on the plateau were reserved and quiet. It didn't mean that they were any less caring—it was just their nature. However, some children had more trouble than others adjusting to this very austere existence.

Generally, Madame Dreyfus found it easier to place younger children than teenagers. Teenage boys were especially hard to place, because they ate so much and they were not as obedient as younger children. One time, she was trying to find a place for two teenage boys and no one would take them in. Finally, at the home of an older couple who had just refused her, she told them the truth—these boys' parents had just been arrested by the Nazis. They were Jews. The couple immediately responded, "Why didn't you say so earlier? Of course we'll take them."

Michel and Jacques, Madame Dreyfus's own sons, were sheltered on the plateau. Their false identity cards gave their last name as Drevet, but they were young and they kept forgetting that. When they were called on in class, their schoolmates would remind them—"Hey, Drevet, the teacher's calling on you!"

In 1943, Madame Dreyfus was arrested and deported to the Bergen-Belsen concentration camp. André Chouraqui, a Jewish refugee living on the plateau, took over her dangerous work. Madame Dreyfus survived eleven months in the Bergen-Belsen camp, and she was reunited with her husband and children after the war ended.

A farmhouse on the plateau. Often the stable and hayloft were part of the house, separated from the family rooms by only a wall.

CHAPTER TWENTY

Two Loving Families
Claude

CLAUDE WAS BORN IN PARIS, *France, on December 21, 1939. When the Nazis invaded Paris he was only six months old. He came to the area of Le Chambon at the age of three, and he was five in 1945, when the Allies achieved victory in Europe. He told us his story at his home in Marseille, France, on April 8, 2004.*

CLAUDE WAS BORN just after the war began. He was sent to live in a tiny hamlet near Le Chambon when he was only a toddler. He has powerful memories of his time there, but because he was very young, his memories are not complete. Much of his story comes from what he was told of his childhood by his two families—his biological family and the loving family that took him in during the war.

CLAUDE'S FAMILY ORIGINALLY CAME to France from Poland, although his father was born in Paris. His parents were Jewish, but they were not religious. The family lived in Paris.

Daniel, Claude's brother, was born in 1942. One day, when Daniel was a tiny baby, Claude's mother was arrested for not wearing the yellow Jewish star. She did have the star. She had sewn it onto her jacket. But it was hot out and she had taken the jacket off. She and her two sons were immediately arrested and sent to the Drancy transit camp.

Many Jews had already been deported from Drancy to the Auschwitz death camp, even children as young as Claude. However, the commandant of the camp told Claude's mother that he had no orders to deport babies. He told them to leave. If Daniel had not been with them, Claude and his mother would both have been sent to Auschwitz, and almost certain death. Claude was only two-and-a-half years old.

After that, the family left Paris.

CLAUDE'S PARENTS NEEDED TO FIND a safe place for their children. They got in touch with a Jewish children's aid organization called OSE (Oeuvre de Secours aux Enfants). OSE found places for Daniel and Claude to live, with farmers in a tiny village just outside of Le Chambon.

Claude had just turned three when he came to live with the Ollivier family.

1943–1945, La Bâtie de Cheyne, France

In order for him to be safe, everyone had to pretend that Claude was not Jewish. But it was very easy for the police to tell whether a boy was Jewish. Jewish boys are all circumcised shortly after birth, and at that time in France, non-Jews were not. To avoid this problem, Claude had to pretend he was a girl! That way, no one would even think to check.

The Olliviers let his hair grow long and taught him to act like a girl. His name had to change, too. Up until now, his parents had called him Louis, his first name. But his middle name, Claude, can be a girl's name in France as well as a boy's name. It was very simple to start calling him Claude or even Claudie. Claude also had to pretend that the Olliviers were his real parents. He was told to call them Mama and Papa, which he did. They were very kind to him, and before long, he forgot that they were not his real parents.

His new family included the Olliviers' daughter, Berthe, who was old enough to help take care of him. His aunt, Hélène, was sheltered by the Olliviers, too. The Olliviers were Darbyists, a fundamentalist Protestant sect. Darbyists truly believed that Jews were God's chosen people, and they felt honored to help them.

CLAUDE WAS VERY HAPPY on the farm. It was small, like all the others on La Montagne Protestante. Every farm had its own animals, fields, and garden. Each family lived on what their farm could provide. There were only a few cows on the Ollivier farm, and they all had names, like pets. Every year the Olliviers raised a pig, which they would slaughter at the end of the year for meat.

Farm children on the plateau, feeding the chickens

Young farmers, getting ready to go out to the fields

Claude remembers that they had chickens, ducks, dogs, and cats. In fact, there were too many cats. He has a vivid memory of seeing dead kittens on the bank of the pond. The farmers would drown the new litters to keep from being overrun by cats.

When the cows were taken out to the fields to graze, Claude went along, too, to help look after them. There were no fences, so the cows had to be kept from wandering away. The dogs were trained to help. In wintertime, the cows stayed inside all the time. The stable with its hayloft was in one part of the house. The family lived in the other rooms.

Every day, the cows had to be milked. The Olliviers let Claude help. He was too young to really be useful, but they let him share in all the chores.

THE FARMHOUSE WAS HEATED by a wood-burning stove. They chopped wood and stacked it all summer. In the winter, the fire burned night and day. They also cooked on that stove. There was a hole on top that could be made larger or smaller, only two sizes, to fit a pot for cooking.

For breakfast, Claude had bread and fresh milk and butter, which they made themselves. They used a wooden butter churn. Claude remembers the women beating and beating the cream in the churn, and then, suddenly, it would become butter. When they took the butter out, a salty liquid was left over. That got fed to the pig.

Everyone on the farm wore *sabots*—wooden clogs. Claude's had a design carved on them. He wore them all year round, even in the snow.

Wintertime was very cold, and there was a lot of snow. The men of La Bâtie dug narrow paths through the snow between the houses so that people could visit one another. They were very isolated. There were only five or six farmhouses grouped together in the tiny hamlet.

One winter, the Olliviers helped their neighbors slaughter a pig. Afterward, they were invited over for a small party to celebrate. Even though he was very young, Claude drank some wine. The wine made him feel sick, so he went outside for some fresh air. He passed out in the snow. He might have frozen to death there, in the snow, if someone hadn't seen him go out. After that, he never drank wine again.

THERE WERE A NUMBER of ponds that the farmers had built using small dams. From time to time, the ponds needed to be emptied for cleaning. Claude remembers very clearly the buckets full of frogs that they collected from the bottoms of the empty ponds. Frog legs are a common food in France. Claude remembers the farmers using scissors to cut the live frogs in half. They probably sold frog legs to other people on the plateau.

Claude made a close friend in the village. Gilbert was about the same age as Claude. In wintertime, they went sledding together. They spent a lot of time collecting rocks. They became fascinated with the many crystals they found. Claude kept his collection in a hiding place out in the fields.

Claude's little brother, Daniel, was living on a farm not too far away. He was not loved in the same way that Claude was, and it was a difficult time for him. But the brothers saw each other frequently and grew very close.

Claude's uncle, who was only three years older than he, lived with another family in the village. In fact, every family in La Bâtie was sheltering at least one Jewish child.

After the war was over, Claude's parents came to bring him home. He had just turned six. He didn't realize they were his parents, even though they had come to visit him often. La Bâtie and the farm were his whole world, he loved the Olliviers, and he had no memories from before his time there. He did not even speak Parisian French anymore. Instead he had learned the regional language spoken in La Bâtie, which was very different. He cried inconsolably when they said he had to leave.

Epilogue

Louis Claude Milgram and his little brother, Daniel, were reunited with their parents in early 1946. Later that year, his sister, Ginette, was born. Claude's parents had survived the war in Lyon, working as vendors in outdoor markets. They had false identities and forged papers. After the war, the family stayed in Lyon, where his parents opened a shop.

It was very hard for Claude to adjust to life with his biological parents. He missed the Olliviers, and his parents were jealous of the bond he had formed with them. He was not able to see the Olliviers again until he was fifteen. From that point on, he visited them often, and he still feels very close to the Ollivier family. He jokes that in his life he has been lucky to have had several mothers.

He met his wife when he was seventeen. They were both in the French Israelite Scout organization, but in different cities. When they became engaged, he took her to meet the Olliviers in La Bâtie. After they married, they went to study in Nancy, France. He became a chemical engineer and his wife worked as a scientist. They have three sons and eighteen grandchildren. They are both retired and live in the south of France.

Madame and Monsieur Ollivier have passed away now, and their daughter, Berthe, lives in Le Chambon. Her son lives in the farmhouse in La Bâtie. Claude remains in close contact with Berthe, and he has been back to the farm many times. He says that he has looked for the rock crystals he hid there many years ago, but he hid them so well that he hasn't been able to find them again.

Claude says, "For me, war didn't exist. I may have traces of the war deep in my subconscious, but consciously, I don't remember it at all. I only remember my life as a part of that family. And it was a very happy life!"

Renée with her younger sister, Edith, in 1939

CHAPTER TWENTY-ONE

A Difficult Adjustment
Renée

Renée was born in the Saarland on February 24, 1931. She was nearly two years old when Hitler became chancellor of Germany and the Nazi party came into power. She came to the area of Le Chambon when she was eleven, and when she was fourteen, in 1945, the Allies achieved victory in Europe. She told us her story when we interviewed her at her home in Garden City, New York, on April 30, 2004.

ALTHOUGH SHE WAS UNDER the age of four at the time, Renée has vivid memories of being taken by the family maid to a parade. Soldiers were lining the street and flags were everywhere. One of the soldiers took her up on his shoulders, and she saw Hitler go by. It was very exciting. When she got home, her parents were furious, and they fired the maid. Renée herself was outraged that they did not understand her excitement or share the enthusiasm of the crowds at the parade. All the homes in her neighborhood except hers flew the Nazi flag. She didn't understand why they couldn't have one, too.

She also recalls that without warning, her friends in the apartment below were no longer allowed to play with her. This occurred shortly after their father came home one day in the brown uniform of a Nazi.

RENÉE'S FAMILY LIVED in the Saarland until 1935, when she was four years old. The Saarland was a small area between Germany and France. It had been created as a separate entity seventeen years before, right after World War I. In 1935, the people of the Saarland voted to become part of Germany. Renée's father understood what that meant for them as Jews. He immediately sold his business, and the family immigrated to France.

Age 8—1939, Sarreguemines, France

I got the Prix d'Excellence, the top prize, at school again this year. That means I'm the best student in my whole class! Last year when I won the prize, Papa asked me what I wanted as a reward. I said, "Two francs." This time, I want a bicycle!

Papa is always listening to the radio. All he listens to is news. When he has the radio on, my little sister, Edith, and I aren't allowed to talk or make any noise. It's so boring.

There are lots of soldiers in town now and tanks in the streets.

Age 8—August 1939, Longeville-en-Barrois, France

I didn't get my bicycle. We had to move instead. Papa's chauffeur drove the truck and Mammie [Mommy] drove the car. Papa can't drive because of his war injuries. He was in a big war back before I was born. There are nine of us in all. Besides Mammie and Papa and Edith and me, Oma [Grandma] lives with us, and my cousins, Lucie and Léon. Their father was killed by the Nazis. And of course there's Sophie, our maid, and the chauffeur.

Age 8—November 1939, Longeville-en-Barrois, France

It's always been my dream to be a Girl Scout. Now I'm in a troop—Les Guides de France. It's the Catholic Girl Scouts, even though I'm not Catholic. We meet every Sunday, and I go to mass with them. Then we go on walks and do other things. I love it!

I really like my school. My favorite thing is when we knit scarves and gloves and socks for our *filleul*—godson. He's a French soldier from Madagascar. Our school adopted him and we send him everything that we knit, plus things like sugar and chocolate. While we're knitting, we take turns reading the Greek myths out loud. It's wonderful! I'm starting to know them all by heart.

On my first day of school, the other kids came over and looked at my head to see if I have horns. They said that Jews are supposed to have horns. I don't think that they had ever met a Jew before. I didn't mind them checking. We're all friends now.

Age 9—February 1940, Longeville-en-Barrois, France

I've been crying all day. They told me I can't be a Girl Scout anymore because I'm Jewish. What does that have to do with being in the Scouts? And I went to mass with them and everything.

Age 9—May 1940, Longeville-en-Barrois, France

Guess what! I have seven cats! There's my kitten, Minou, but also a stray cat wandered in, and last week she gave birth to five more kittens! I'm feeding them, because the mother cat leaves them to go hunting every day. So I have to take care of them. They're so little and sweet.

EVERY TIME THERE'S AN AIR RAID, we have to go down into the cellars to be safe. There isn't a cellar under our school, so we stop class and run to the houses nearby. Everyone says prayers, Ave Marias and Paternosters.

Age 9—Late May 1940, Bar-le-Duc, France

We're in jail. I had to leave all my kittens behind. Who will take care of Minou?

Two *gendarmes*—policemen—came to get Edith and me from school. We were in the cellar with the other kids during an air raid. The gendarmes brought us home. Mammie was trying to pack for all of us: Edith and me and Mammie and Papa and Oma and Lucie and Léon. Sophie, the maid, left us last month, so Mammie had to do it all herself. The gendarmes said she only had fifteen minutes.

They put us in a truck and brought us here. Mammie said that they arrested us because they think we're German spies. They searched us to see if we were hiding anything. They undid our hair and looked under my sister's curls. They even searched us between our legs. It was awful.

They've put us in the stables, except for Papa and Oma. Papa can't lie down on the floor because of his war injuries, and Oma is eighty-four years old. It's very hot in here, there are rats, and the smell is horrible. We're right next to the latrines.

We've been here for days. I miss Minou. I hope the kittens are okay.

Age 9—June 1940, en route to Gurs internment camp, France

We've been on this train for seven days. Papa bought some drinking water from the soldiers. We each have half a piece of bread, but Papa says we have to save it for the morning. So we will have no dinner.

The train is filled with people like us, from the prison. It's very crowded and we can't bathe. Our whole family is crammed into one compartment. At night, Léon sleeps on the floor, and Mammie, Papa, and Oma have to sleep sitting up on the wooden benches. Lucie and I sleep with our heads on Mammie and Oma's laps. Edith is small enough to fit up in the baggage net, so she sleeps up there.

At first, the soldiers gave us a little food and water, but after the second day, they stopped. My parents tried to buy food each time the train came to a station, but no one would sell them anything. We couldn't understand it. Then, we found out why. One day, they let us off the train for a few minutes. "Prisoners of War" was painted on the side of our train in big letters. That's why everyone hates us—they all think we're German spies being taken to prison!

There's nothing to do but look out the train window. There are red poppies and blue bachelor buttons growing in the wheat fields, and it is so beautiful. Yesterday I saw the sea for the very first time.

Age 9—July 1940, Gurs internment camp, France

The ground is so muddy here it's like clay. Edith and I use it to make little sculptures and marbles. Sometimes they give us soup with chick peas in it for dinner, but the chick peas aren't cooked enough. They're so hard, we can use them as marbles, too.

There are no trees here at all, just mud. There are barracks as far as you can see, one row after another. The only nice thing to look at are the mountains way off in the distance.

Mammie is calling us. They've turned on the water for a little while. She wants us to wash, and she's going to wash our underpants. We only have one pair each, so Mammie washes them every day. It's not raining today, so they'll dry more quickly than they did yesterday. That's a good thing. Yesterday, while I was waiting for them to dry, a lady came and admired my dress. It's the only one I have now. Mammie knitted it for me and that's what I was wearing when we were arrested. The lady began to pick up the hem to look at the stitches more closely. I was afraid she would lift it all the way up. I was so embarrassed!

Mammie insists on keeping us as clean as she can. She says that's why we don't have dysentery like all the other kids here.

There are fleas here, and bedbugs. Rats run across our faces at night. Everyone has lice, even us, and they make our scalps itch. Some people came and put stuff on our heads to get rid of the lice. It worked, but it really burned. Edith and I got huge blisters on our heads. It hurt so much!

In our barrack, there are only mothers and children. They come from all over. There are even some Gypsies. The grown-ups try to stay away from the Gypsies. I don't think they like them.

Papa is in the hospital here. Every day, Mammie takes us to see him. It's a long walk and it's very hot during the day. The doctors are nice. Whenever we come, they have treats for Edith and me— hard-boiled eggs, preserves, and, once, even chocolate.

Renée (right), in her little knit dress, with Edith in the Gurs internment camp

Age 9—September 1940, Villeurbanne, France

Papa got us out of Gurs and we moved here, to a suburb of Lyon. Now we are living in a skyscraper, in a big empty apartment. We hardly have any furniture. They keep turning off the electricity, so we use candles at night. It's just the four of us again. Oma and my cousins are on their way to America to live with my uncle. Last night, Mammie made our first home-cooked meal in a long time. Soon we start school. I can't wait!

Age 10—July 1941, Villeurbanne, France

Edith and I go to the Ecole Anatole France. I love my school. At the beginning of every day we raise the flag and sing a hymn to Maréchal (Marshal) Pétain. He's the leader of Vichy France. We all write letters to him, and he writes us back. I even got a medal from him once. I was so proud.

Age 11—July 1942, Villeurbanne, France

I wish I could just sink into the ground and disappear. I'm so ashamed to be Jewish. All the students are here, lined up in the school yard. It's the end of the school year and they're giving out prizes. The school director was announcing the winner of the grand prize for good sportsmanship and academic performance. She said that I had been selected, but that she was sure that the Maréchal would not want such an important prize to go to someone of my race. She means Jewish. Instead, she awarded the prize to Monique Gaz, my rival! I can't believe it. I'm so ashamed. Two of my teachers came to comfort me, but it only made me feel more embarrassed. It's awful to be Jewish.

Age 11—July 1942, Le Chambon-sur-Lignon, France

Mammie said Edith and I have to go away for a little while. She took us to Lyon to make arrangements with a nice lady named Madame Dreyfus. A few days later, Edith and I left with Madame Dreyfus for Le Chambon. She told me not to talk about who we are or where we're from. She said I could write to my parents, but they wouldn't be writing back.

When we arrived in Le Chambon, a family was there to meet Edith, but no one was there for me. I'm spending the night with Madame Déléage. She's responsible for finding places for children like me.

Age 11—August 1942, Le Chambon-sur-Lignon, France

I hate it here. This farm, La Souche, is in the middle of nowhere.

It's just me, Monsieur and Madame Fournier, and their son, Marcel. There's no electricity, and we get our water from a pump outside. The cow and the goat drink from the same trough that we use when we wash. The Fourniers had never even seen a toothbrush before I came. On Sunday mornings, they wash and dry their feet at the pump. Then they use the same towel to pat dry the goat cheese they've made. It's disgusting.

Every morning after breakfast, Marcel and I take the cow and the goat to graze. Marcel guides the cow by hitting her on the backbone with a stick. It makes such a dreadful sound! The goat does what she wants and isn't guided so easily.

I like to sit by the stream and daydream. Sometimes I make necklaces out of ferns and fronds. The ferns in the forest are taller than I am. I think they're beautiful.

There's nothing to do here. There are no books, except the Bible. There's

La Souche, as it is today. The trough, which was the only source of water, would have been at the left. Otherwise the farmhouse looks very much the same as it did when Renée was there in 1942.

no wool to knit, nothing. Madame Fournier is kind to me, and Marcel is nice, too, but I'm very lonely. I've never been away from Mammie and Papa and Edith before, and I miss them so much. If only there was a cat here, then maybe I could stand it.

THREE GIRLS FROM ST. ETIENNE are living here with us now. They sleep with me in the kitchen alcove. Even though they're about the same age as me—eleven—they never talk to me. And I'm not supposed to tell anyone who I am, so I don't talk to them much, either. I'm still lonely.

Monsieur Fournier took me to visit my sister yesterday. She's staying with a family in Tence, nearby. She's very happy there. The family has a son her age and they play together.

Last night, Monsieur Fournier told me that all of the Jews in Lyon had been arrested and that I would never see my parents again. He's always saying horrible things like that. Why can't he be as nice as Madame Fournier? Every time he says something, I twitch. Lately I've started to twitch even when he's not talking to me. I can't stand it here.

Age 11—August 1942, Villeurbanne, France

I feel like crying. I ran away. I walked through the woods to Tence by myself to get my sister. I used up all my money taking the train back home to Villeurbanne. But my parents aren't here! I don't know where they are and I don't know what to do.

THE NEIGHBOR HEARD ME CRYING and told me where Mammie and Papa were. They've been hiding in another neighbor's apartment. All the Jews in the neighborhood have been arrested except them. Mammie says we have to go right back to see Madame Dreyfus. She doesn't want us to stay here one more minute.

Age 11—August 1942, Le Chambon-sur-Lignon, France

Madame Dreyfus didn't make me go back to La Souche. She brought me to stay with the Mesdemoiselles (Misses) Royal. There are a lot of other girls staying here, too. They must be relatives of the Royals, but I'm not sure. We never mention our last names.

I share a room with three other girls. They're really nice. My sister sometimes comes to visit. She's back with the family she stayed with before.

It's not so bad here. There are books and an indoor bathroom. We don't have very many chores. We just make our own beds and help set the table. We're close enough to town that I can walk to the post office. I send postcards to Mammie and Papa.

I play a lot with the other girls. We were exploring and we found a tree covered with little black berries. We tried them and they tasted good, so we ate more. I guess we ate too many because we all got terrible stomachaches.

One day, the Mesdemoiselles Royal told us that Vichy inspectors would be coming and that we had to go out to the fields for the day. Yesterday, the inspectors came back. We were in the middle of lunch, so we had to sit and eat our cream of leek soup while they watched. I hate cream soup, but I ate it all.

Age 11—September 30, 1942, Villeurbanne, France

We're going to Switzerland. Madame Dreyfus brought Edith and me back from Le Chambon and now we are all getting ready to leave. Mammie and Papa have false identity papers with new names on them. We are no longer the Kanns, now we are the Webers. We have to memorize our new names, and we can't take anything with us that has our real names on it.

Age 11—October 1, 1942, Annecy, France

Mammie is really upset. We are trying to calm her down. We were waiting in the back of this restaurant for a guide to take us across the border to Switzerland. He finally arrived, and he told us that yesterday forty-five people were

Renée's parents' false ID cards, showing their name as Weber

arrested at the border and sent to deportation camps. He's asking for extra money to guide us across.

IT'S PITCH DARK OUT HERE. There are only the four of us, and we've been walking through the fields in the dark for hours. The guide pointed to a light off in the distance and told us to go there, that the people there would help us, and that then we would be in Switzerland. But we've been walking for a long time, and some more lights came on, and then some others went out. Now we have no idea where to go.

Mammie and I are carrying all the bags. Edith is helping Papa. It's hard for him to walk through the fields, even with his cane. He fell down once, but somehow managed to get up again and find us. He couldn't call to us for help. We're afraid to make any noise.

All the lights have gone out but one. We're heading toward it.

Age 11—October 1, 1942, Switzerland

A dog is barking. We have reached the courtyard of a farm. A woman comes out and invites us in. We're very lucky, she says. The border patrol has just passed. She gives us hot cocoa and bread. She says we can't stay there, but sends us to an empty house nearby and brings us warm blankets.

Age 11—October 2, 1942, Switzerland

When we woke up this morning, a family across the street invited us to have breakfast with them. They were very nice to us. Soon we'll get on the train to Basel. I think I'm going to like it here.

Epilogue

Renée Kann and her family stayed in Switzerland until the end of the war. They returned briefly to Sarreguemines, where they found that the town had been devastated by the war. Their only relatives who had survived the war were those who had immigrated to the United States. When Renée was sixteen, the family moved there, too, settling in Pennsylvania, near Renée's cousins, Léon and Lucie. By that time, her grandmother was no longer alive.

Renée was fluent in French and German and had four years of Latin. She attended high school for one year, where she perfected her English. During her first year of college, she met her husband, an American World War II veteran. They married two years later, when she was nineteen years old.

She used her talent for languages, working for many years as a teacher of French, Spanish, and English.

Renée Kann Silver and her husband live in New York. They have one son and three grandchildren.

Renée's sister, Edith, married and had four children. She lives in Florida.

Renée says, "Le Chambon was a very difficult period for me. . . . It was the first and only time I was separated from my parents. . . . I really had kind of put Le Chambon out of my mind."

Many years later, she read an article in the newspaper about Weapons of the Spirit, *a documentary that was being shown on the subject of Le Chambon. She contacted two people named in the article and learned that it was indeed a film about the town where she had been sheltered as a child. Then, she says, ". . . a few years later, there was a reunion in Le Chambon. Not only about the rescuers and the survivors, but the Resistance movement in Le Chambon in general. And I had gone there and Pierre Sauvage's movie* [Weapons of the Spirit] *was shown there for the first time and some of the people in it were still alive. It was wonderful! And that's when . . . [my husband] . . . and I took out a topographic map and found La Souche."*

Students sledding to class. Sometimes they made a train of sleds, using their feet to hold on to the sled behind.

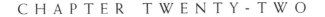

CHAPTER TWENTY-TWO

Sledding to School
Jacqueline

Jacqueline was not a Jewish refugee. She came to Le Chambon during the war to study there. We interviewed her at her home in Etival, France, on April 9, 2004.

THE ECOLE NOUVELLE CÉVENOLE was such an excellent school that some children came to Le Chambon to study, even during the war. Jacqueline, a fourteen-year-old French Protestant from Lyon, was sent by her parents in January 1942 to Le Chambon to study there. She lived at Le Colombier, a *pension*—boardinghouse—for female students. She came home for the holidays, taking the very slow train from Le Chambon. The train climbed hills so slowly that she was able to get off the train, gather daffodils while the train paused to build up steam, and get back on, as it continued up the hill.

Le Colombier was run by a devout Protestant woman named Madame Marion. She ran a tight ship and everyone had to be punctual. Early each morning, she'd ring a bell when it was time to get up. Another bell would signal breakfast. At breakfast, they had coffee with milk, but it wasn't real coffee. Sometimes it was made from carrots, cut into small pieces and grilled. Sometimes it was made of chicory or other roasted grains. They called it "ersatz" coffee, and it always tasted terrible! From time to time a little real coffee would be mixed in, but real coffee was scarce during the war.

All the girls at Madame Marion's wore *sabots*—wooden clogs—with thick socks all winter long. The sabots felt heavy in the summer, so they all went barefoot.

Madame Marion and the girls at Le Colombier, spring 1943.
Jacqueline is the fifth from the bottom, sitting on the steps in between a blonde girl and a girl standing against the column.

Le Colombier in the snow

Madame Marion was very frugal, but she was also very generous when it came time to help someone in need. When the daughter of an imprisoned *maquis*—Resistance fighter—needed a place to stay, Madame Marion found room for her, even though the pension was already full. She also took in Jewish refugees.

Although she was not Jewish herself, Jacqueline had many Jewish friends and housemates. One of her classmates was arrested in a raid at La Maison des Roches. Sometimes her Jewish friends who were hiding in Le Chambon with their parents invited her to visit them, so that she could enjoy being in a family atmosphere. They were warm and welcoming to her. However, she could tell that they were worried about other members of their family who were hidden elsewhere. Where were they hiding?

Had they been arrested? What was happening to them? They didn't know. One of her friends never did find out what happened to his father. He simply disappeared.

She also knew that some refugees were secretly leaving for Switzerland. Everybody talked about it but in very low voices. One time, Jacqueline found out that a whole group of kids from Faïdoli who had been guided to the Swiss border had to turn back because they couldn't get across.

Jacqueline knew about the maquis. The brothers of some of her friends had joined the maquis, and there was a constant fear that they might be arrested or killed.

At the Ecole Nouvelle Cévenole, Jacqueline remembers sledding from class to class during the winter. She would have history class in a house above the village, then everyone, even the teachers, would pile onto sleds and *whoosh* down to English class at the Protestant temple. The room there was freezing, so they would stoke the stove. But the stove would smoke so badly, they would have to open the windows. Then it would be freezing again!

Some of Jacqueline's teachers were Jewish refugees. One of them was very generous about loaning books to all of his students. He and his wife would invite the students to their house, and they would discuss what the students were reading. When Jacqueline was sick, and missed several months of school, he loaned her lots of books to read in the infirmary.

Jacqueline always felt welcome when she visited her friend Nelly Trocmé at the *presbytère*—the pastor's house. Nelly's parents, Pastor André and Magda Trocmé, had a constant flow of students, refugees, and friends streaming through their house. The dinner table was often full of company. The Trocmés were warm and spirited, and the presbytère echoed with music and poetry.

Jacqueline and her friends managed to enjoy themselves, in spite of the war. The girls at Le Colombier sometimes threw parties. At Mardi Gras, they liked to have costume parties. One time some of them made fun of the German army by dressing up in army uniforms and goose-stepping along, giving the German military salute!

Jacqueline graduated from the Ecole Nouvelle Cévenole and returned to Lyon. She became a clinical psychologist and married a doctor. They settled in Lyon. Jacqueline and her husband have five children, eleven grandchildren, and a great-granddaughter.

One of the Rivières wood-burning trucks. René learned to drive in a truck just like this one.

CHAPTER TWENTY-THREE

A Family in the Resistance

René

René was not a Jewish refugee. However, he lived in Le Chambon and went to school there during the war. We interviewed him at his home in Le Chambon on November 11, 2002, and on April 6, 2004.

RENÉ, A FRENCH PROTESTANT, was ten years old when the Nazis occupied France in 1940. His earliest memory of the injustice of the war concerned the principal of his school in St. Etienne. The principal was an extraordinary man, someone the students respected and looked up to. But, suddenly, one day he was fired from his job because he was Jewish. He and his family had to leave their home. They had nowhere to go.

The school was across the street from René's family's business, and René saw the principal, his wife, and their three children standing in front of the school with one small suitcase for all of them. René was horrified to see such a dignified man so humiliated. René's aunt Dora took the family in, and they lived with her in her mother's house.

During the war, René and his family came to stay in Le Chambon, where they had a country house. His parents felt that it would be safer for him there. His father continued to run the family transportation business in the city of St. Etienne. Although St. Etienne was only about forty-five miles away, it was a long trip. The train was slow. It took five or six hours to go from St. Etienne to Le Chambon.

Because of the war, gas was scarce. Some French people modified truck engines so that they could run on wood or charcoal instead of gas. When René was twelve years old, he learned to drive using a truck powered by two wood-burning boilers, mounted one on each side, with sacks of wood piled in the truck for fuel. Later on, when American soldiers saw those peculiar trucks, they laughed and laughed.

You needed special authorization to travel by car. There were very few cars on the roads, and they were stopped often by the *gendarmes*—police—to check that they had the proper authorization.

Many people traveled by bicycle. René remembers seeing nuns riding by on their bicycles, their habits billowing out behind them. Because tires were hard to find, sometimes people would carry their bicycles partway, so the tires would last longer.

René started at the Ecole Nouvelle Cévenole in the middle of the school year, but he was not the only one. During the war, it was a common occurance there, because of the arrival of so many refugees. No one was made to feel like an outsider.

Many of the students joined the Scouts, and they often knew one another by

Boy Scouts out fishing on the plateau

the totem name of their troop. Some of the foreign refugees' names were difficult to pronounce. It was a lot easier to use the totem names.

René took Italian with Magda Trocmé, the wife of the pastor. She held class at her kitchen table, and the students had to peel carrots and potatoes while she taught them Italian. Sometimes she would send René on an errand, but he didn't always understand what she asked him to do, because she only spoke in Italian during class. Sometimes, she would send him out for carrots and he would come back with potatoes!

In Le Chambon, René stayed at Les Heures Claires, a *pension*—boardinghouse— for boys who were students at the Ecole Nouvelle Cévenole. Every Sunday, the boys went to services at the Protestant temple. A group of girls from another pension also went to services there. It was a good meeting place!

The traditions of La Montagne Protestante made it the ideal place that it was for welcoming refugees. The people shared their homes and shared their food. René remembers that at Boy Scout camp, everyone brought what food they could, and it all went into a common supply. Some boys had nothing to contribute, but the food was shared equally among them all.

Members of René's family were actively helping refugees. René's aunt, Dora Rivière, a doctor and a feminist, was in the Resistance. She also hid many Jewish refugees in her home. One of those refugees was Jakob Lewin (*see* Chapter Eleven, "I'll Fight Back: Jakob"), who hid there for several weeks with his brother, Martin, and a friend. In addition, working with an organization called Aid to Mothers, Madame Rivière found hiding places for many Jewish women and their children. She was arrested in 1944 and deported to the Ravensbrück concentration camp. She survived the horrific conditions there and came home after the war.

René's father, Henri, sheltered Jewish refugees, too. They often stopped at his home in St. Etienne, on their way to Switzerland. He also used his business to transport weapons for the *maquis*—Resistance fighters. After René's Aunt Dora was arrested, his father had to go into hiding as well. René's father spent nearly a year living secretly with the Dolmazon family on the plateau. They were a devoutly religious family. Monsieur Dolmazon later said that the most difficult thing for him was having to teach his children to lie. He told them that if anyone asked whether there was someone hiding in their house, they must say no.

Today, René Rivière and his wife live in Le Chambon.

Daniel Trocmé in 1939

Tragedy
Daniel Trocmé and
La Maison des Roches

DANIEL TROCMÉ CAME TO LE CHAMBON when his cousin, Pastor Trocmé, asked him to run Les Grillons. A young man, he had been offered a teaching job elsewhere. However, he wanted to do more. There was a war going on. He wrote his parents: "For me, Le Chambon will be first an education, but also some kind of contribution to the reconstruction of our world."

Les Grillons was a home for refugee children between the ages of ten and seventeen. Daniel Trocmé was devoted to the children. He did everything he could to take care of them, from finding them clothing to getting some of them false papers. He had the *sabotier* make them *sabots*—wooden clogs—and in the summer, he made them sandals out of old tires.

Even though he was already busy at Les Grillons, he agreed to run another

La Maison des Roches

home in Le Chambon. La Maison des Roches was for older students, young men who were refugees from the French internment camps. They came from all over: Germany, Poland, Austria, Russia, Hungary, Lithuania, Romania, the Netherlands, Spain, Czechoslovakia, Iran, Belgium, Luxembourg, France, and Tonkin (now Vietnam). About half of them were Jewish.

A few months after he took charge of La Maison des Roches, tragedy struck. Early in the morning of June 29, 1943, the Gestapo—Nazi secret police—surrounded the house. They interrogated every student there. Daniel Trocmé, who spent his nights at Les Grillons, was brought to La Maison des Roches by some of the Gestapo. He had been warned that they were coming for him, and he could have escaped, but he stayed. He felt his place was with the students. Magda Trocmé came and tried to help. She was able to save one of the boys from being arrested. In the end, eighteen students were arrested, along with Daniel Trocmé. All of them were deported. Five Jewish

Students at La Maison des Roches relax on the terrace.
[Chambon Foundation]

students arrested that day at Les Roches died in Auschwitz. As for the rest, seven survived the war, and the fate of six others is still unknown.

Up to the very end, Daniel Trocmé remained devoted to the children and young men in his care. Even from prison, and then from the French internment camp where he spent several months before being deported, he was eager for news about them. He wrote his parents asking them, "How is each little Grillon?" He asked his parents to convey his love to them. He was not allowed to write to anyone but his parents, so he enclosed a note to the children in one of his letters, asking his parents to pass it along. In it, he wrote: "My greatest joy will be to see you all again. It will be magnificent. I will be back with you as soon as I possibly can. You can count on that."

Daniel Trocmé was never able to fulfill his promise. He died in the Maidanek death camp on April 4, 1944.

A group photo taken at Les Grillons in the summer of 1943. Daniel Trocmé is in the back, on the right. His cousin, Pastor André Trocmé (rear, center), is visiting Les Grillons. Peter Feigl (see Chapter Fifteen, "Sabotaging the Nazis: Peter") is in the back row, second from left. [Chambon Foundation]

Joseph (on the right) and his twin brother, Victor, in Le Chambon in 1942

CHAPTER TWENTY-FIVE

The Bad Boy of La Guespy

Joseph

JOSEPH WAS BORN IN WARSAW, *Poland, on September 15, 1926. He was twelve years old when the Nazis invaded Poland and World War II began. He came to Le Chambon when he was fourteen or fifteen, and he was eighteen years old when the Allies achieved victory in Europe. He told us his story at his home in Paris, France, when we interviewed him on November 14, 2002.*

Age 11—Summer 1938, Warsaw, Poland

Everybody keeps telling Mamo [Mom] that good Jewish mothers wouldn't send their young sons so far away. But she has decided to send my twin brother, Victor, and me to boarding school in France. She says that with all the anti-Semitism, there's no future here in Poland for Jews. Tato [Dad] agrees. Since she goes to

Paris every year, Mamo asked her friends there if they knew of a good school for us. They told her about the school in Fontainebleau. She says it's next to a forest, which is healthy, and it's an elegant school. Exactly what she was looking for.

My brother and I each received three big packages from the school, full of everything we'll need there. The school caps have gold braid.

Age 12—September 30, 1938, Paris, France

Victor and Mamo and I just got here. We are on our way to Fontainebleau. Our hotel is near the Gare du Nord train station. There are huge cheering crowds at the station to welcome the French premier back from his meeting with Hitler, Mussolini, and Chamberlain. Everyone says that now there won't be a war.

Age 12—October 1938, Fontainebleau, France

Mamo brought us here to school, but then she had to return right away to Warsaw, because she works with Tato in the family business. Victor and I are going to stay here for the whole school year, even through the holidays.

Age 12—September 1939, Arcachon, France

Germany has invaded Poland! Tato and all my relatives are still in Warsaw. Mamo came to get us as soon as school ended. But Tato had to stay behind to run the business. Mamo brought Victor and me here to the south of France. Right now we're staying in a fancy hotel. Soon, we're going to go live in Paris for a while.

Age 13—October 1939, Paris, France

It's been two months, and we haven't heard anything from Tato or our relatives in Warsaw.

Age 13—December 1939, Paris, France

We finally got a letter from Tato. He wrote that he was happy to know that we were not in the Jewish ghetto in Warsaw, where he is.

Age 14—November 1940, La Drome, France

I don't like it here. We're living in a very small house, the three of us. My brother and I go to the local public school now. I do odd jobs to try and make a little money. Mamo is working as a maid in other people's houses. We're surviving.

After the Nazis invaded France last May, we had to leave Paris. Because we're Polish citizens, we went to the Polish consulate in Lyon to ask for their help. They sent us to the Polish Red Cross, who sent us to stay in a small hotel here in La Drome. But after a couple of months, the hotel manager kicked us out. He denounced us to the authorities. He said we're not Polish, we're Jewish, and he won't let us stay. So now we're on our own.

Age 14—April 1941, La Drome, France

The *gendarmes*—police—are here. We're under arrest! They said we have one hour to pack our things. We are packing as fast as we can.

WE HAD TO LEAVE ALMOST everything behind. They would only allow us to take a few small packages. The gendarmes said that we are foreign refugee Jews, and so we have the lowest Jewish status in France. Polish Jews are no longer under the protection of the Polish government.

Age 14—June 1941, Gurs internment camp, France

I'm always very hungry here. We never get enough to eat, and all of us have lice. It's disgusting! Whenever it rains, the whole camp is under nearly a foot of water—the dirt here is like clay, and the rain doesn't soak in. We have no electricity, no water, not even beds. We sleep on straw on the floor in wooden barracks. Victor and I are in the men's barracks, but we're allowed to visit Mamo in the women's barracks.

Everything has happened so quickly since the war started. But now I understand the situation. Not my situation, *the* situation. I realized how things were when I saw Mamo yesterday, her hair unwashed and her dress so worn,

The interior of a men's barrack in the Gurs internment camp, 1941

and looking terribly thin and weak. She's changed so much since we've been in this internment camp.

I have to get out of here and find us some help.

Age 14—July 1941, en route, Toulouse to Gurs internment camp, France

I did get out, but I really have no choice. I have to go back. The Polish Red Cross gave me a train ticket back to Gurs. They said that if I tried to escape from France on my own, then Mamo and Victor would never get out of the camp. But if I did return to Gurs, they would help us.

When I left Gurs, I didn't have any identity papers or money. I watched the guards marching around the camp with their guns, and when I saw my chance, I slipped under the barbed wire and escaped from Gurs into the night. I snuck onto a train headed for Toulouse. I had to hide in the bathroom on the train because I didn't have a ticket. In Toulouse, I found the Polish Red Cross office and asked for protection as a Polish citizen. I told them that I was not a Jew. They gave me permission to stay for two nights, but they told me I couldn't stay any longer than that. They said that the Polish Red Cross is an official organization, and that I broke the law when I escaped from Gurs. They won't help us unless I go back.

Age 14 or 15—September 1941, Gurs internment camp, France

After six months, my brother and I are finally getting out of Gurs! A group of us are being sent to a village called Le Chambon. There are seven of us going. Everyone is about my age. No adults are allowed to go, so Mamo will have to stay behind. We leave for Le Chambon tomorrow.

Age 14 or 15—September 1941, Le Chambon-sur-Lignon, France

We've been here for a week. I arrived in Le Chambon with nothing, only the clothes I was wearing. The villagers here have given me some old clothing. It is humiliating.

Victor and I are living in La Guespy, a home for refugee kids. Hanne (*see* Chapter Twenty-six, "Love in Wartime: Hanne and Max"), Jakob (*see* Chapter Eleven, "I'll Fight Back: Jakob"), Willi, Lilli, and Mannfred, who came with us from Gurs, are living here, too. La Guespy is run by Swiss Aid for Children, but it is really run by Mademoiselle Usach. Mademoiselle Usach is very small, and I think one of her legs is shorter than the other. She's the director of the house, and we don't get along at all.

Compared to Gurs, Le Chambon is a paradise. Five or six of us share each room, but we all get real beds. And after Gurs, the food is wonderful—cheese, potatoes, carrots, bread.

But for me it's not a paradise at all, because Mamo is still in Gurs, and the rest of my family is still in the Warsaw ghetto, and we've had no news.

Age 15—November 1941, Le Chambon-sur-Lignon, France

There are some nice people here at La Guespy. One of my roommates is Alexandre Grothendieck. He's a math genius, and he's always working on complicated projects. I really admire my friend, Jean Nallet (*see* Chapter Sixteen, "In the Maquis: Jean"). He's two years older than me. He's here with his sister.

Age 16—1943, Le Chambon-sur-Lignon, France

Mamo is here in Le Chambon. She was in Gurs longer than us, and now she's finally here. She works for the Trocmé family at the pastor's home three days a week. She helps with the sewing and other chores. I visit when she's there. Sometimes I play football with the kids. I like them, but sometimes I feel em-

Teenage boys from La Guespy. Joseph is sitting on the far right. His brother, Victor, is on the far left, and Rudi Appel (see Chapter Six, "Lighting Hanukkah Candles: Rudi") is second from right, in front.

barrassed around them—they're the children of the most important person in Le Chambon, Pastor Trocmé, and I'm just a poor Jewish refugee kid.

I speak Polish with my brother. I speak German with the other refugee kids, and I speak French at school. But Madame Trocmé insists that I learn Italian, too. I get along very well with her. She teaches Italian at my school, the Ecole Nouvelle Cévenole. It's a private Protestant school with very high standards. Madame Trocmé is Italian, and she is very distinguished and beautiful. She's also very tough. She puts everyone in his place and not even the president of the republic would dare disobey her!

Madame Trocmé says I need to learn Italian romantic poetry. I'm very bad at it. She tells me sometimes in class, "[Joseph] Atlas, you are an idiot." But it doesn't upset me, because it's just her way of speaking. What bothers me is that I just can't seem to learn Italian. Otherwise, I'm a very good student. Better than Victor, who has to go to the local public school.

TODAY I HAD WHITE CHOCOLATE for the very first time. It was delicious! Monsieur Bohny gave us all some. He's now in charge of the Swiss Aid homes in Le Chambon. He gets huge cheeses from Switzerland for us. Even so, I'm hungry a lot. I'm very tall, and I need a lot of food. Sometimes I get so frustrated that I run around and around the house shouting, "I'm hungry! I'm hungry!"

ON MONDAYS, I LIKE TO GO to the Protestant temple. Every week, Pastor Trocmé gives a speech there especially for young people. You don't have to be Protestant to go.

None of the villagers have ever asked me what my religion is and there's never pressure to become a Protestant. Everyone is accepted without any fuss. And no one talks about it.

Some of the children of La Guespy, with Mademoiselle Usach on the right. Joseph, the "bad boy" of La Guespy, is second from left.

Age 16—1943, Le Chambon-sur-Lignon, France

I saw my school report today. My teachers said that I'm serious and I work hard and I'm intelligent, but they also said that I'm very critical and rebellious. I guess I'm a fighter. I have a reputation now as the "bad boy" of La Guespy. I'm always making trouble. Sometimes it just makes me angry when I'm sitting in class and I look around at all the well-dressed students who can afford to pay for school. I'm here on charity and I hate it. My whole life depends on other people. Nobody in my family has ever depended on anybody. I feel so ashamed and so angry.

GOOD THING I'M IN the Scouts. My troop, the Jaguars, built some small tree houses out in the woods, high up in the trees. When the gendarmes came to Le Chambon to arrest Jewish refugees, I hid in one all night long.

I've had to hide several times. This summer, the gendarmes were in Le Chambon a lot, and it was too dangerous for me to stay in town. Madame Trocmé brought me to a small and very poor farm to live for a while.

The farmers had three cows. My job was to take the cows out to the fields each day. At that time of year, there are millions of biting flies and they wouldn't leave the cows alone. The cows ran all over the fields trying to get away from the flies, and I couldn't catch them. I'm not meant to be a farmer!

Age 16—August 1943, Le Chambon-sur-Lignon, France

I saved a man's life today. He's a German. I don't know his name because I ran away before his friends could stop me. If they knew I was Jewish, it would be dangerous. I didn't even know he was German when I jumped into the river to save him. But it wouldn't have made any difference. I would have done it anyway.

Sometimes the German soldiers who are staying at the hotel in town come and swim in the same spot in the river as all of us refugees. The only difference between us and them is that they wear black shorts to swim in. Today I saw that this man was drowning, and I jumped in without thinking and pulled him out of the water. He must have had a cramp.

The Lignon River, on the edge of Le Chambon

When all the other German soldiers rushed over, I realized he was one of them. So I ran. I didn't want them to ask who I was.

Age 17—Summer 1944, Le Chambon-sur-Lignon, France

One of my school directors got mad at me, and they wanted to kick me out of school. When the school rented a bus to take us to Le Puy-en-Velay for our Baccalauréat exams [final exams to graduate from high school], they wouldn't let me ride on the bus. I was really upset about that. Le Puy is sixty-five kilometers away, and if I didn't take the exam, I wouldn't be able to go to a university. So I rented a beat-up, old bicycle.

Partway there, I caught up with the bus. It had stopped to wait for me. Some of my friends had convinced the director to let me ride with them. But I said, "I will not go with you!" I didn't need their bus! And I bicycled the whole way there, up and down all the hills.

I was tired when I got to Le Puy, but I did just fine on the exam—and I graduated!

EPILOGUE

Joseph Atlas left Le Chambon with his mother and his brother, Victor, after the war ended. They learned that nearly all of their family had perished in the Treblinka death camp.

Joseph attended a university in France, where he got his degree in chemical engineering. He says, "Generally speaking, the French population was anti-Semitic but not active. People in the cities were under the influence of anti-Semitic propaganda [during the war]." He felt that many in the Vichy government, which was responsible for the active anti-Semitism in France, remained in power after the war ended. He and his mother and brother chose to immigrate to South America, rather than live in France. They lived in Santiago de Chilé for a number of years, where he and Victor had their own business.

Joseph visited Paris often. He met his wife there, a French Jew whose parents were also originally from Poland. He and his mother moved back to France when he married. Victor still lives in South America. Joseph Atlas and his wife have lived in Paris since 1965. His mother lived with them until she passed away.

During the course of his career, Joseph traveled throughout the world. He and his wife have worked as volunteers for many years helping to obtain pensions for French Jews who had been persecuted by the Vichy government during the war. In 2004, the president of France, Jacques Chirac, awarded Joseph Atlas the title "Chevalier de l'Ordre de la Légion d'Honneur," a very high honor in France.

Joseph never forgot Le Chambon. He learned that it was thanks to Pastor Trocmé that he and other young people were released from Gurs and sent to live in Le Chambon. He says, "At Gurs, they destroyed people; the cemetery has more than one thousand Jewish graves. André Trocmé saved our lives. There was intensity and intelligence in his blue-eyed gaze, he was a great orator, and he spoke vividly of his convictions from the pulpit; and the people acted on them. All the people of the plateau protected, sheltered, fed, and clothed us, with the help of Swiss Aid for Children. We survived thanks to them."

He also says, "The Ecole Nouvelle Cévenole was, for me, an opening, and determined my future life because the teachers there, and especially the Protestant pastors, gave me a moral and ethical sense of things. . . ."

Hanne in 1936, in a studio photograph taken by her mother,
and Max in 1934, at the time of his bar mitzvah

Love in Wartime

Hanne and Max

HANNE WAS BORN IN KARLSRUHE, *Germany, on November 28, 1924. She was eight years old when Hitler came to power, and nearly fourteen years old on* Kristallnacht— *the Night of Broken Glass. She came to Le Chambon when she was sixteen. She was twenty when the Allies achieved victory in Europe.*

Max was born in Mannheim, Germany, on September 3, 1921. He was eleven years old when Hitler came to power, and seventeen years old on Kristallnacht. He came to Le Chambon when he was twenty. He was twenty-three when the Allies achieved victory in Europe.

Hanne and Max told us their stories at their home in Bayside, New York, when we interviewed them on February 22, 2003.

Max, Age 8—1929, Mannheim, Germany

I'm starting cello lessons soon. I just turned eight, and now I'm big enough to play. My teacher is in a real orchestra. I can't wait!

Hanne, Age 5—1929, Karlsruhe, Germany

I hope Mama doesn't catch us. She told us to stay inside the apartment, but my brother, Alex, and I want to see. We're out on the balcony again, watching down below. A lot of people are yelling and fighting in the street. I don't know what they're fighting about. Alex says it's political. He's eight years old, so he knows.

Max, Age 11—April 1, 1933, Mannheim, Germany

Brown Shirts—Storm Troopers—are standing guard in front of all the stores that are owned by Jews. They're keeping everybody from going in. They've put up signs everywhere telling people not to buy from Jews. Why are they doing this to us?

Max, Age 12–13—1934, Mannheim, Germany

I've learned an important lesson: You can't walk away from trouble, you have to face it. Once the Nazis came into power, the kids in my class kept pushing me and the other Jewish kids around. There are only four of us. They taunted us and shoved us and wouldn't leave us alone. Finally, last week I decided I'd had enough. I was furious. I picked a boy I thought I could handle, and I really gave him a beating. None of the other kids helped him. They just stood around and watched me beat him up. Ever since then, they've left us alone.

Max, Age 14–15—1936, Mannheim, Germany

I've started lessons with a new cello teacher. My first teacher chickened out and dropped all his Jewish students. He was afraid he would lose his position in the orchestra. My new teacher has a little more courage.

A Jewish chamber orchestra was organized last year, because the Mannheim

April 1, 1933—the first Nazi boycott of Jewish-owned businesses in Germany. Storm Troopers are keeping everyone from going into this store, which is owned by Jews. One of the signs reads: "Germans, defend yourselves against the Jewish atrocity propoganda, buy only at German shops!"

Theater Orchestra was no longer permitted to perform for Jews. I'm going to play cello in the new orchestra.

Max, Age 16—1937, Mannheim, Germany

I'm through with school. It's gotten worse and worse because many of the teachers are Nazis and all the kids are in the Hitler Youth. I'm sixteen years old, but as a Jew, I wouldn't be allowed to go to university or to a music conservatory, anyway, so what's the point?

My friends and I never tell our parents about what goes on. They have enough problems as it is.

Hanne, Age 12–13—1937, Karlsruhe, Germany

We can't play with anyone who isn't Jewish, but I don't care. I have lots of Jewish friends. Jews are not allowed to go to theaters, concerts, movies, restaurants, or the swimming pool, but the man who's in charge of the pool lets us sneak in sometimes. He says we have to disappear before ten o'clock, when the pool opens. You can bet we're out of there before ten! We don't want to get him in trouble, and besides, then we couldn't use the pool anymore.

We like to ride our bicycles in the Black Forest nearby and have picnics. At least when we're in the woods, no one is shouting, "You stinking Jew!" at us like they do in town. Sometimes, when I feel brave, I say, "Yes, I am a Jew, and *you* stink!"

ALEX LEFT FOR AMERICA TODAY. He's sixteen. Papa died when I was a baby, so now it's just Mama and me and Grossmutter [Grandmother].

Max, Age 16—March 1938, Mannheim, Germany

Pappa is gone. He had to leave Germany to try to find work. I remember when I was young, he had a big office with lots of people working for him. Now his business is closed because the people he used to work with aren't permitted to do business with Jews. He's gone to Greece to see if he can find work there. Mamma and I have given up our apartment to save money and moved in with Grossmama [Grandma].

Max, Age 17—Kristallnacht, November 10, 1938, Mannheim, Germany

I was lucky today. I could have been arrested. The Nazis were going crazy, burning and looting Jewish homes and arresting all the Jewish men. I managed to slip out and spent the day in Heidelberg, where no one knew me.

Hanne, Age 13—mid-November 1938, Karlsruhe, Germany

One day last week, the Nazis went on a rampage against Jews. They smashed all the showcases in Mama's photo studio, but they left our apartment alone. Maybe they didn't feel like walking all the way up to the fourth floor. Anyway, there were no men up here for them to arrest.

A sign posted on a telephone pole in a German town reads: "Jews are not welcome here."

Now they want all of our silverware and jewelry—anything that's valuable. They're making us turn it all over to them. The only thing we're allowed to keep is Mama's gold wedding band.

MAMA'S REALLY BUSY. A new law says that all the Jews in Germany must carry identification cards. She's taking photos all day long to put on the cards.

Max, Age 18—September 1939, Mannheim, Germany

Germany is at war! I'm eighteen, so I had to report to a Nazi army office along with all the other Jewish men. We were sent east to help farmers with the harvest. We worked hard every day for weeks, and when the harvest was done, I was sent back home. All that work was for free— they never paid any of us.

Things have gotten much worse since the war started. Food is rationed. Jews get less than everyone else and are only allowed to shop for one hour a day. We can't own cars, telephones, or radios, and we're not allowed out of our homes after dark.

Max, Age 18—Summer 1940, Mannheim, Germany

A lot of Jews have been trying to leave Germany. I've been working since January 2 for the emigration office that helps them. It's not easy, but we've helped a lot of people.

Hanne, Age 15—September 1940, Karlsruhe, Germany

Today Mama said that if we cannot take everything with us when we go, the one thing she wants is her piano. And I said to her, "One day, we will leave without the piano." She got really mad and told me to stop saying things like that.

Adults think that all this will blow over, and they tell us not to get so upset. My friends and I know better. I remember standing on our balcony and watching the Nazi soldiers marching in the streets. They were singing, "When Jewish blood spurts from the knife, then things go twice as well." I knew then that things were really bad. And it's only gotten worse.

Hanne, Age 15—October 22, 1940, Karlsruhe, Germany

The Gestapo—Nazi secret police—are here. When Mama went out this morning, someone told her we were all going to be deported, all the Jews in the city. She rushed back home and began packing frantically for us. Grossmutter is ninety-two years old and needs help. We're only allowed to bring what we can carry, and we have to bring food and blankets as well as clothing. For money, we're only allowed to bring one hundred reichsmarks each.

She told me to take some of our best things to her friend Erika, and when I got back, the Gestapo were here. I whispered in Mama's ear what Erika had told me, that she had heard we were being sent to the south of France. Mama didn't believe me. She was afraid that we would be going to a German concentration camp or maybe to Poland.

Hanne, Age 15—October 24, 1940, en route to Gurs internment camp, France

Erika was right. When we crossed the border into France, everyone was somewhat relieved. But now we're still on the train and it's been two days, and we have no more food or water. This is all too much for my poor Grossmutter. I think she's losing her mind.

Max, Age 19—January 1941, Gurs internment camp, France

Mamma and I have been in this internment camp since we were deported last October. Every Jew in our province was sent here. Gurs is huge. The whole camp is surrounded by barbed wire, and each block of barracks is, too.

During the first few days, I never got to see Mamma. The men and women live in separate barracks. The only way to leave your block is with a pass, but they're hard to get. Shortly after arriving, I started working in the office of my block, helping to organize things here, and I can get a pass almost every day. I go to see Mamma, who is working in her block's office. Working is a good way to pass the time. It's better to stay busy.

Gurs is filthy. The straw we sleep on is filled with bugs, and there are rats everywhere. We have to wash ourselves outdoors at a big trough, and they only turn the water on for a few hours. Of course, there is no hot water, even in the winter.

Many people here, especially the older ones, have had a very hard time getting used to Gurs. It's such a shocking change from our former lives. We're given very little food. Some have starved to death. Others are weak, and lots of people have dysentery or typhus. Part of my job in the office is to report on the number of people who have died. A man comes in every day to take away the bodies.

Hanne, Age 16—January 1941, Gurs internment camp, France

Mama and I thought we were lucky to be deported to the south of France, but Gurs is horrible. People die here every day. At least at the funerals, husbands and wives get to see each other. The rest of the time they have to live apart—right at a time when people need to be together the most!

I work in the block office, handing out mail and running errands. I've learned how to count in French. The woman I work for has a son. Max is nineteen, three years older than me. He comes to visit his mother here almost every day. He's tall and handsome. I like him a lot.

We've started walking over to the Swiss Aid for Children barrack together every morning. They give the young people extra food so that we won't starve to death. We get things like dried milk and olives and cheese and halvah, but we have to eat it there. We can't take any food back with us. Our group goes for extra food for four weeks, then another group gets a turn. Max and I get to talk while we walk over and back. I think he really likes me, too.

Max, Age 19—August 1941, Gurs internment camp, France

My girlfriend, Hanne, has a chance to get out of Gurs. Swiss Aid for Children is planning to take some people to a village called Le Chambon. Hanne doesn't want to leave her mother behind, but they can't take any adults. I've encouraged her to go, even though I'll really miss her. Seven teenagers were given permission to leave, but then the Polish twins, Joseph (*see* Chapter Twenty-five, "The Bad Boy of La Guespy: Joseph") and Victor, went missing. Everyone has to wait until they are returned to Gurs.

Hanne, Age 17—March 1942, Le Chambon-sur-Lignon, France

Seven of us came here from Gurs together—me, Jakob (*see* Chapter Eleven, "I'll Fight Back: Jakob"), Mannfred, Willi, Lilli, and the twins, Joseph and Victor. We get along pretty well, although the twins are always fighting with each other. We live with some other refugee kids in La Guespy, a group home run by Swiss Aid for Children. Mademoiselle Usach is in charge. She doesn't particularly care for girls. I am the oldest girl here.

When we got here, Elisabeth (*see* Chapter Four, "Lost: Elisabeth") came from the Trocmés to help us. She's a Jewish refugee from Vienna, and she was taking care of the Trocmé children. Most of us didn't speak French, and Elisabeth was fluent. I liked her. She stayed with us for a while, but she's gone now. She's lucky, she got a visa to go to the United States.

At first there was so much food, compared to Gurs, that we couldn't eat it all. We toasted some of the bread we were given and sent it to our friends and

An elderly woman imprisoned in the Gurs internment camp uses a stick to keep her balance, while walking in the deep mud in the camp.

families in Gurs. Now that we've been here awhile, it seems like there's never quite enough to eat.

One day, Madame de Félice asked us to help pick fruit from her orchard. She told us not to eat any, and that she would give us some later. But we couldn't wait. We sat in the trees, stuffing ourselves with apples and plums!

Now that we understand some French, we sometimes go to the Protestant temple on Sundays. We don't have any radios or newspapers, so we never know what's going on. I don't think Pastor Trocmé likes it that we come, because no one here wants to convert us to Christianity. We don't go for the service, though. We go to find out what's happening outside of Le Chambon. We're always thinking of our loved ones in Gurs.

Max, Age 20—March 1942, Gurs internment camp, France

There are some very famous musicians interned here at Gurs. The YMCA (Young Men's Christian Association) has sent us musical instruments, and we've set up a string quartet. I've heard the entire violin and piano sonatas of Beethoven, played by the most talented musicians in the world. Such a magical experience in such a horrible place as this!

Hanne, Age 17—August 6, 1942, Oloron-Sainte-Marie, France

The train is leaving. Mama is on it. Everyone is crowded into freight cars. Jakob's parents are there, too, and so many others. A thousand people are being deported from Gurs.

I don't know where they're taking them, but Mama told me she didn't think she'd ever be coming back.

I had gotten a pass to visit Mama in Gurs, because she was ill. But when I got here, they wouldn't let me in to see her. The whole camp was locked down and no one could come in or out. We saw each other through the barbed wire, but we were so far apart we had to shout.

Early this morning, I went to the freight yard at Oloron. They were loading everyone onto the freight cars. I got to see Mama for about an hour. Then they took her away.

Hanne, Age 17—August 1942, en route to Le Chambon-sur-Lignon, France

I went directly to see Max after I left Oloron. Two weeks ago, he was released from Gurs and sent to a farm run by the Jewish Boy Scouts. I'm so glad he got out of Gurs in time. He was very upset about the deportation. His mother is still in Gurs.

I told him that if he thinks he's not safe on the farm, he should come to Le Chambon, where I am.

Now I have to go back to La Guespy and tell the others.

Hanne, Age 17—August 1942, Le Chambon-sur-Lignon, France

Mademoiselle Usach has gone away for a little while. She left me and Monsieur Steckler in charge. We've heard that there are going to be roundups. I don't think we should stay here at night. It's not safe. I'm taking everyone to sleep at L'Abric, because Monsieur Bohny lives there. He's in charge of all three Swiss Aid homes, and he will take care of us.

Max, Age 20—August 1942, Le Chambon-sur-Lignon, France

A few days after Hanne came to see me, we found out that the gendarmes were coming to raid the Boy Scout farm, and that we would all have to hide. I left with Walter, my friend from Gurs, and we came to Le Chambon to find Hanne.

We slept in the woods overnight. When we woke up, we heard some girls talking and I recognized Hanne's voice! She told me that they were walking back to La Guespy after spending the night at L'Abric.

We went with them to La Guespy, and then Hanne took me to see Madame Philip. She's in the Resistance. She was able to place me on a farm nearby where I could hide.

I've been hiding here for two weeks. I stay in the hayloft all day and night. The toilet is in an outhouse, but I can't go out there because I might be seen. So the farmer cut a hole in the floor of the hayloft for me to use as a toilet. The only time I leave the hayloft is when I eat dinner with the farmer's family. They give me a lot of food, and I'm getting my strength back.

I just got a note from Hanne. It's good to know I haven't been forgotten here.

Hanne, Age 17—August 1942, Le Chambon-sur-Lignon, France

I'm so glad Max is here in Le Chambon. Madame Philip will help him.

I was right to bring everyone down to L'Abric every night to sleep. The gendarmes did come to arrest us, but Monsieur Bohny insisted that they had no right to do so. He told them the house was under Swiss protection. They questioned each of us. Then they said that they would be back in the morning, and that Monsieur Bohny was responsible for keeping us there until then. And they left.

As soon as morning came, Monsieur Bohny sent us into the woods to hide. We spent the day there gathering blueberries, since we had no food with us. They were delicious! In the evening, Monsieur Bohny sent someone to get us, and then we were all taken to different farms.

I've been here for two weeks already. I'm in hiding with one other girl. We don't even know the name of the farmer who's hiding us. We're way out in the country, and the farmer's dog barks every time a stranger approaches. A few times, the gendarmes have come looking for us. But every time, we heard barking, and we knew we had to hide in the woodpile.

Max, Age 21—September 1942, in the French Alps

It's nighttime, and I'm sitting as far back as I can under this rock overhang, trying to stay out of the rain. I'm exhausted. We spent all day climbing up the mountains, and once the rain started we got soaked. A ten-year-old boy is guiding us. He knows the way over the mountains to Switzerland. A Protestant pastor named André Morel has come along to learn the route from him, so that he will also be able to guide people over the border to safety. There are four of us trying to get to Switzerland.

I spent four weeks hiding on the farm near Le Chambon. Then Madame Philip got me a false identity card and told me that I would be guided to Switzerland along with three other young men. We took the train to the mountains. The boy who is guiding us met us in St. Gervais. Tomorrow we should reach Switzerland. Now we have to try to sleep in the cold and the rain.

THIS MORNING, AT THE TOP of a ridge, the boy told us it would be easy from there—all we had to do was climb down and we would be in Switzerland. Then he and Pastor Morel turned around and headed back. On the way down, I buried my false identity card, just like Madame Philip said I should. She was afraid that if I were caught with it, the border guards would realize I was being helped by a rescue organization. That could endanger the whole rescue effort. Now the only ID I have is my German identity card marked with a big *J* for Jewish.

The slope was so rocky that my shoes were torn to shreds. It's a good thing I had a spare pair in my backpack. I never would have made it down in bare feet. We're in Switzerland!

As we walk down the road, we suddenly hear voices behind us. Someone yells, "*HALT!*" We turn to look. It's the Swiss military police.

The swiss police had been watching us through their binoculars for hours. They've caught many people during the past day, all of us trying to escape into Switzerland. They have food for us, but they're making us pay for it. That's the last of my money. They say that in the morning they're going to take us all back up into the mountains, and we must return to France.

I have to try to go back to Switzerland again. I'm trying to convince the others. When the border guards led us up here, one of them kept telling us in a loud voice, "DON'T do that, DON'T go there," and then they left us here to continue on our own. But as he was talking, I realized he was actually giving us clues on how to get back into Switzerland. All we had to do was take out the "DON'Ts" and we would know just how to do it. I think he was trying to help us, but no one else seems to understand.

Anyway, I can't go back to France. I don't have my false identity card anymore, and I could never find it again, buried under the rocks.

I've finally convinced one other man to come with me. Everyone else is going back to France.

Hanne, Age 17—September 1942, Le Chambon-sur-Lignon, France

The roundups are over for now and the gendarmes are no longer bothering us. We are all back at La Guespy. But I don't feel safe here anymore. Max has gone to Switzerland. I think we should all go.

Hanne, Age 18—February 26, 1943, Le Chambon-sur-Lignon, France

I have my false identity card. It says I was born in Paris. I have a visa for Switzerland from my aunt who lives there. But I have no exit visa to leave the country, so I will have to sneak out of France.

I have my briefcase with a toothbrush, a nightgown, and a towel. I'm also bringing a couple of pieces of cheese and some bread, because I have no ration card and won't be able to buy any food. I'm wearing two skirts, two blouses, a sweater and a cardigan under my coat. This is all I'm taking to Switzerland. I'm ready to go.

Hanne, Age 18—February 28, 1943, en route to Switzerland

Guess who was on the train! Monsieur Bohny! He rode with me all the way to Lyon, then he had to go back. Lyon was full of German soldiers. I took another train from Lyon to Annecy, near the Swiss border. In Annecy, I was supposed to spend the night at a convent. They told me in Le Chambon that the nuns would help me. But it was late when I got there, and no one answered the door. I found a cheap hotel where they wouldn't ask too many questions about my identity papers, and I spent the night there.

This morning, I went back to the convent, and they gave me coffee and bread for breakfast. They didn't ask me to pay, but I left some money for them, anyway, hidden under a cup. They were very nice. They told me to catch a bus to Annemasse, which is very close to the border, and then walk from there.

Hanne, Age 18—February 28, 1943, at the Swiss border

I've reached the border. I hope I don't have a problem with the Swiss guards—I have a legal visa to get into Switzerland. I'm anxious about the French border police, though, because I don't have permission to leave France. If I can just get into Switzerland, I think I'll be safe. I'm just going to keep walking.

CARTE D'IDENTITÉ

Nom _Husser_

Prénoms _Anne-Marie_

Profession _Etudiante_

Née le _3 avril 1925_

à _Paris IX_

Département _Seine_

Domicile _25 boulevard Buyeaud Oran_

Nationalité _Française_

SIGNALEMENT

Taille _1 m 69_

Cheveux _Blonds_

Moustache

Yeux _Bleu gris_

Nez _droit_

Visage _ovale_

Teint _clair_

Signes particuliérs _néant_

Empreinte digitale :

Pièces justificatives fournies
ou signatures des Témoins :

1° _Déclaration conférant la qualité de française le 17 février 1926 N° 17.307_

2°

TIMBRE
de LÉGALISATION

Oran le : 14 DEC 1939

Hanne's false identity card, made for her in Le Chambon

A FRENCH CUSTOMS OFFICIAL has stopped me. He wants to see my papers. I'm acting confident and showing him everything I have. I hope he doesn't ask me anything about Paris, my supposed birthplace. I've never even been there!

He looks me straight in the eye and says, "Are you Jewish?" I wasn't expecting that. Without thinking, I reply, "I have nothing to do with this dirty race!" And he lets me through!

Max, Age 21—March 1943, Sierre Labor Camp, Valais, Switzerland

Hanne made it to Switzerland, too! She's living with her aunt and uncle, and I can't wait to see her. They give me three days' leave every six weeks here.

This labor camp is really not so bad. No barbed wire, no guards, and we even get paid for our work. It's not much, but at least it's pocket money.

Hanne, Age 20—April 14, 1945, Geneva, Switzerland

Today Max and I are getting married!

Max in the Sierre labor camp in Switzerland

Epilogue

Johanna (Hanne) Hirsch Liebmann and Max Liebmann lived in Switzerland for several years, helping to run various refugee camps. Their daughter was born in Switzerland in March 1946.

Max learned that his mother had been deported from Gurs in November 1942 and perished in Auschwitz. His father, who lived in France during the war, was arrested in 1944, two weeks before D-Day, and deported to Auschwitz, where he was killed. The last time Max saw his father was when he left for Greece in 1938.

Hanne never saw her mother again. Her mother was deported to Auschwitz and died there. Hanne's brother, Alex, had enlisted in the U.S. Army and was killed in action in 1945, in the Battle of the Bulge.

Hanne, Max, and their young daughter came to New York City in March 1948, with seventy dollars in their pockets. Max found work immediately. In 1950, both Max and Hanne contracted tuberculosis and had to be hospitalized for months. When they recovered, Max went to business school briefly, where he studied accounting. He went on to a successful career in business, retiring as vice president of his company. In retirement, he continues to work as a volunteer. He has played the cello with many different groups throughout his life.

Hanne visits schools and libraries, where she gives talks about her wartime experiences.

The Liebmanns have stayed in touch over the years with many of the people they met in Gurs and Le Chambon.

Max says, "You have to understand one thing. We were all children when Hitler came to power, but by the time we came to Le Chambon, we were no longer children."

Hanne says, "It's very much in the Jewish tradition to help another. . . . But I think the people in Le Chambon went a lot further, under the most difficult circumstances. . . . The people were just so wonderful to us. It was a unique experience to be in that place, really and truly, it was unique."

She adds, "I have an elderly friend, she is ninety-two. . . . She got sick and Max and I picked her up . . . [and] took her to a . . . hospital and it was back and forth. And I spoke to her sister-in-law who thanked me profusely, and I said, there is no need for that. . . . Listen, I said, there was a time in my life [when] other people helped me, so now I'm helping someone else!"

A view of modern-day Le Chambon [Chambon Foundation]

Epilogue

A VISITOR TODAY to La Montagne Protestante, now known as the plateau Vivarais-Lignon, will find that the village of Le Chambon-sur-Lignon has changed over the years, although it is still primarily Protestant. The words carved over the temple door still urge all who enter, *Aimez-vous les uns les autres*—"Love one another." The train station where so many children disembarked still stands, but the only trains that arrive now are tourist trains in the summertime. The pension Beau Soleil that was run by Madame Barraud is now a hotel, rather than a boardinghouse. The Ecole Nouvelle Cévenole, now called the Collège Cévenol, still attracts students from all over the world, but now they have their own campus.

The plateau is still a popular vacation spot, especially for people who like the outdoors. Many of the farmhouses have been converted to vacation homes. The woods have spread, and now there are fewer fields than there were. The winters are not as harsh as they used to be, but the Lignon River still flows past and daffodils still cover the hillsides each spring.

Over the years since the end of World War II, refugees of other wars have sought shelter on the plateau. People from many different countries, even as far away as Tibet, have found welcome there. Le Chambon is now an official center for political refugees seeking asylum in France. At this writing, forty men, women, and children are living in Le Chambon, waiting to be granted political asylum. The adults are being taught French, and, just like during the war, the children go to school in the village. La Montagne Protestante—the plateau Vivarais-Lignon—continues its tradition of offering refuge to those in need.

WHEN PEACE CAME TO the plateau after World War II, the refugees left. Despite the generous spirit of the people who sheltered them, the war years had been very traumatic. Many of the young refugees had become orphans. Some of them had relatives to go to, but some had nobody at all. Many refugees had to begin life again with nothing.

They left the plateau behind them. It was a long while before many of them really began to understand everything that had been done for them there. Even then, some still didn't talk about it.

Over the years, some of the former refugees came back to the plateau to thank the people who had saved them. For some people, this was many years in coming. Others maintained close ties. Pierre Bloch's family always returned to the plateau for their family vacations. Even now, although he lives in Israel, he considers himself a "Jew-Huguenot" of Le Chambon.

In 1979, a group of people who had been sheltered in the area put up a bronze plaque in honor of the inhabitants of the plateau. The plaque is in Le Chambon, and faces the Protestant temple where Pastors Trocmé and Theis led their services.

For a long time, the people of the plateau didn't talk about what they had done,

Marie Brottes with Jewish refugees Bubi and his father, Doctor Mautner. Monsieur Brottes is on the left. [Chambon Foundation]

not even to one another. Parents didn't even tell their children. Marie Brottes' son, Jean, didn't know that refugees had been hidden in his mother's home. He wondered why a box of chocolates arrived for his mother from Austria every year, since she had never been out of Le Chambon. He would ask her, but she would only reply, "You may have some chocolates, but you shouldn't ask questions. It's none of your business." Finally, after the plaque was placed in Le Chambon, thirty-four years after the war, Madame Brottes told Jean her story for the first time. As she reached the end of her life, she also told her grandchildren about the role she had played. She hoped that by passing on the story she could influence future generations, and perhaps stop new persecutions from taking place.

All over Europe, Jews were hidden by small groups and brave individuals. But La Montagne Protestante was unique in Europe. For the four years of the Nazi occupation of France, almost the entire population of eight thousand people worked actively toward the same goal: saving Jews from destruction. Not a single inhabitant of La Montagne Protestante ever betrayed any of the refugees. By the end of the war, they had saved at least three thousand five hundred Jews, as well as about one thousand five hundred other refugees.

Yad Vashem, Israel's museum of the Holocaust, awards a medal to those it calls "Righteous Among the Nations." It is given to non-Jewish people who saved the lives of Jews during the war. As of 2005, Yad Vashem had awarded the "Righteous Among the Nations" medal to sixty-four people on the plateau, including pastors, farmers, charity workers, and others, both adults and teenagers. In 1988, Yad Vashem awarded the medal to all the inhabitants of Le Chambon-sur-Lignon and the surrounding communities. This was the first time the medal had ever been given to a group rather than to an individual.

Not all the refugees have been able to say thank you. Some didn't know the names of the people who had hidden them, and some had been too young to remember. Some had a very difficult time while they were there. Although their lives were saved by being on the plateau, it took them many years to come to terms with their experiences. Others never knew the exact location of the farm that sheltered them, or they had passed through so quickly that they would never be able to find it again.

But the people of the plateau never required thanks. They didn't consider themselves to be heroes. At the time, they didn't talk about what they were doing. They simply acted, without feeling that they were doing anything extraordinary. In their minds, they were simply doing what was right—the normal, decent thing. Sometimes, however, doing the normal, decent thing is heroic.

In the midst of the overwhelming darkness of the Holocaust, the story of La Montagne Protestante is a powerful testament to the goodness of the human spirit.

POSTSCRIPT

As of 2005, sixty-four people on the plateau had received Yad Vashem's "Righteous Among the Nations" medal. Many of them are included in this book. They are:

Madeleine Barot, 1988

Gabrielle Barraud and her mother, Georgette Barraud, 1988

Pastor André Bettex, 1988

August Bohny, 1990

Friedel Bohny-Reiter, 1990

Marie Brottes, 1989

Samuel Charles, 1993

Pastor Daniel and Suzanne Curtet, 1990

Roger Darcissac, 1988

Léonie Déléage and her daughter, Eva Déléage Philit, 1988

Pastor Charles Delizy, 1988

Pastor Marc and Françoise Donadille, 1986

Léon and Antoinette Eyraud, 1987

Louise and Arthur Franc, 1999

Mayor Charles Guillon, 1991

Henri and Emma Héritier, 1987

Pastor André Morel, 1990

Jean and Nancy Ollivier, 1989

Mireille Philip, 1976

Pierre Piton, 1989

Pastor Edouard and Mildred Theis, 1981

Pastor André Trocmé, 1971

Daniel Trocmé, 1976

Magda Trocmé, 1984

Juliette Usach, 1989

Le Chambon-sur-Lignon and the surrounding communities, 1988

GLOSSARY

Allies The Allied nations during World War II were the four most important nations to help fight the Axis nations, or the enemies. The Allies were the United States, France, Great Britain, and the Soviet Union. The Axis nations were Germany, Japan, and Italy.

Brown Shirt Another name for Storm Trooper (*see* Storm Trooper)

camps The Nazis set up concentration camps, where people were imprisoned under brutal conditions; labor camps, where people were forced to work at hard labor while they were imprisoned; and death camps, where they were sent to be killed. All of the camps were horrific, and many people died in each of them. The largest of the camps, Auschwitz, was both a concentration camp and a death camp; at the death camp, most of the people were killed by poisonous gas and then cremated. Nearly 1.5 million men, women, and children were killed in Auschwitz. Almost all of them were Jewish.

In France, there were also internment camps run by the French, where people were sent to live. In addition, there were transit camps, where people were held temporarily until they could be deported to death camps. Drancy was a transit camp in France. Nearly everyone who came to Drancy was deported to Auschwitz to be killed.

After the war, camps were set up for "displaced persons"—the survivors who had lost their homes and families. These were places set up for people to adjust to conditions after the war, and they stayed until they could find a new place to live.

collaborator Someone who cooperates with the enemy

D-Day June 6, 1944, the day the Allied forces began their invasion of France. This led to the end of the war.

deportation During the war, Jews and others were deported—this meant that they were sent away to concentration camps or to death camps to be killed.

fifth column Undercover spies from another country. During World War II, the fifth column were German spies sent undercover to France and other countries.

The Final Solution of the Jewish Question The Nazi plan for the mass murder of Jews, including children, which began in June 1941. Often it was simply called the Final Solution.

Free French Army French soldiers who continued to fight against the Germans after France fell to Germany. The Free French Army also fought against Vichy France.

gendarmerie A French police station. A gendarme is a French police officer.

Gestapo The Nazi state secret police. Gestapo is short for *Geheime Staatspolizei*. The Gestapo were particularly brutal. They arrested and tortured many thousands of people.

Hitler Youth This organization was created in Germany in 1926 to train young boys to become Nazis. In 1939, all German boys between ten and eighteen years of age were required to join the Hitler Youth.

The Holocaust The mass slaughter of six million Jews and many others by the Nazis and their followers during World War II.

Kristallnacht The "Night of Broken Glass." In Germany, on November 9–10, 1938, approximately ninety-one Jews were killed, nearly every Jewish male aged eighteen to sixty-five—thirty thousand men—was arrested, almost all of the synagogues were burned down, and over seven thousand Jewish businesses were looted and destroyed by the Nazis. Because of all the shattered glass in the streets, this rampage came to be known as Kristallnacht.

Nazi The political party of Germany, led by Adolf Hitler, which was in power from 1933 to 1945. It is an abbreviation for *Nazionalsozialistische Deutsche Arbeiterpartei*, which means National Socialist German Workers' party.

SS The SS (Schutzstaffel—Protection Squad) was a special section of the Nazi army. Originally bodyguards for Hitler, the SS became extremely powerful and developed into the Nazi party police. SS soldiers were specially trained. They were responsible for carrying out the Final Solution, and they ran the concentration camps.

Star of David The six-pointed star that is the symbol of the Jewish religion, also called a Jewish Star.

Storm Trooper Storm Troopers were also called Brown Shirts, after the color of their uniforms. The Storm Troopers, or SA (short for *Sturmabteilung*), were a separate Nazi army, made up of average German citizens.

swastika The swastika was originally a good luck symbol. Its name comes from Sanskrit. The Nazis adopted the swastika as their official symbol.

Warsaw Ghetto In 1940, Jews in the Polish city of Warsaw were forced by the Nazis to construct a ghetto by building a wall that would seal them in. The Nazis forced Jews to live in ghettos throughout eastern Europe. The ghettos were horrible places to live, overcrowded and filthy, and many people died of starvation and sickness. The word *ghetto* is originally an Italian word. It was first used in Italy in the 1500s, to refer to an area where Jews were forced to live apart from the rest of the people in the city of Venice.

"When Jewish blood spurts from the knife, then things go twice as well." This was a chant sung in celebration by the Storm Troopers in 1935 when they were marching.

yarmulke A skullcap worn by observant Jewish men

yeshiva A religious Jewish school

PRONUNCIATION GUIDE

L'Abric—lah-breek

Aimez-vous les uns les autres—em-may-voo layz-uhn layz-oh-truh

Auschwitz—OWSH-vits

Barot, Madeleine—bah-row, mah-duh-len

La Bâtie de Cheyne—lah bah-tee duh shen

Beau Soleil—boh soh-lay

Besson, Daniel—beh-sawn, dahn-yell

Bettex, André—beh-tex, ahn-dray

Blut und Ehre—bloot oond AIR-uh

Bohny, August—bow-nee, oh-goost

carte d'identité—kart dee-don-tee-tay

Le Chambon-sur-Lignon—luh shahm-bawn-sir-leen-yawn

château—shah-toe

CIMADE—see-mod

Le Colombier—luh koh-lohm-bee-ay

Le Côteau Fleuri—luh ko-toe flur-ee

coupon réponse—coo-pawn ray-pawn-ss

Curtet, Daniel—cur-tay, dahn-yell

Dachau—DAH-hhow ("hh" sounds like clearing your throat)

Darcissac, Roger—dahr-see-sock, roh-zhay

Delizy, Charles—duh-lee-zee, sharl

Devesset—duh-vuh-say

Donadille, Marc—dawn-ah-dee-uh, mahrk

Drancy—drahn-see

Dreyfus, Madeleine—dry-fooss, mah-duh-len

Ecole Nouvelle Cévenole—ay-cole new-vel say-vuh-nole

Ein Volk, Ein Reich, Ein Führer—ine FOHLK, ine RYEHH, ine FEWR-uhr ("ine" as in "fine" and "hh" sounds like clearing your throat)

Faïdoli—fah-ee-doh-lee

Fay-sur-Lignon—fah-ee-sir-leen-yawn

filleul—fee-yule

Fräulein—FROY-line

Freycenet—fray-suh-nay

gendarme—zhon-darm

gendarmerie—zhon-darm-air-ee

Gestapo—guh-SHTOP-oh

Les Grillons—lay gree-awhn

La Guespy—lah geh-spee ("g" as in "get")

Guides de France—geed duh frawn-suh ("g" as in "geese")

Guillon, Charles—gee-awn, sharl ("g" as in "geese")

Gurs—gurz

heil—hile (rhymes with "pile")

Henri—awn-ree

Jacqueline—zhah-kleen

Jakob—YAH-kub

Jean—zhawhn

Juif—zhew-eef

Kristallnacht—KREESS-tahl-nahhkt ("hh" sounds like clearing your throat)

Léon—lay-awhn

lingère—lahn-zhair

Lise—leez

Madame—mah-dahm

Mademoiselle Usach—mah-duh-mwah-zell oo-zah-sh

Maidanek—MY-duh-neck

La Maison des Roches—lah may-zawhn day roh-sh

maquis—mah-kee

Maréchal Pétain—mah-ray-shahl pay-tanh

Marthe—mahrt

Le Mazet—luh mah-zay

Mesdemoiselles—may-deh-mwah-zell

Les Milles—lay meel

Monsieur—muh-ss-yuh

La Montagne Protestante—lah moan-tahn-yuh pro-tuh-stahnt

Montbuzat—mawn-boo-zah

Morel, André—mawh-rell, ahn-dray

Mutter—moot-tuhr

Mutti—moot-tee

OSE—oh-zay

passeur—pah-sur

pension—pawn-see-awn

Philip, Mireille—fee-leep, mee-ray-uh

Piton, Pierre—pee-tawn, pee-air

Poivre—pwahv

presbytère—prez-bee-tair

prestataire—press-tah-tair

Prix d'Excellence—pree dex-sel-awn-ss

razzia—(the R is rolled) ROT-see-uh

Résistance—ray-zis-tawn-ss

ribambelle—ree-bom-bell

Rivesaltes—reeve-salt

sabot—sah-bow

sabotier—sah-bow-tee-ay

St. Cyprien—san sip-ree-enh

Tante Soly—tahnt so-lee

Les Tavas—lay tah-vah

Theis, Edouard—tice, ed-warh

Trocmé, André—trawk-may, ahn-dray

Vater—fah-tuhr

Vati—fah-tee

Le Vernet—luh vair-nay

Les Versas—lay vair-sah

Vichy—vee-shee

Le Vigiant—luh vee-zhee-awn

Vivarais-Lignon—vee-vah-ray-leen-yawn

Waldi—VAHL-dee

weeshuis—VAYSS-how-ew-ss

yarmulke—YAHM-uh-kuh

yeshiva—yuh-SHEE-vuh

RECOMMENDED READING
THE HOLOCAUST RESCUE EFFORT IN LE CHAMBON-SUR-LIGNON

BOOKS AND ARTICLES

For children and teenagers:

Kustanowitz, Esther. *The Hidden Children of the Holocaust: Teens Who Hid from the Nazis.* New York: Rosen Publishing Group, 1999. This nonfiction book for teenagers includes the story of a girl who was sheltered in Le Chambon. It is part of the "Teen Witnesses to the Holocaust" series.

Leapman, Michael. *Witnesses to War: Eight True-Life Stories of Nazi Persecution.* London and New York: Viking/Penguin, 1998. This nonfiction book for teenagers includes the story of a girl who was sheltered in Le Chambon, as well as seven other true stories of the Holocaust.

Matas, Carol. *Greater Than Angels.* New York: Simon & Schuster Books for Young Readers, 1998. This novel for young teens is based on the experiences of several of the hidden children of Le Chambon.

Steiner, Connie Colker. *Shoes for Amélie.* Montréal: Lobster Press, 2001. This illustrated chapter book for young readers tells the fictionalized story of a hidden child in Le Chambon.

Zapruder, Alexandra, ed. *Salvaged Pages: Young Writers' Diaries of the Holocaust.* New Haven: Yale University Press, 2002. This compilation, appropriate for teens and adults, includes excerpts from the diaries of two hidden children of Le Chambon, Elisabeth Kaufmann Koenig and Peter Feigl.

For adults:

Fogelman, Eva. *Conscience & Courage: Rescuers of Jews During the Holocaust.* New York: Anchor Books/Random House, 1995. There are many references to Le Chambon in this book.

Hallie, Philip. *Lest Innocent Blood Be Shed: The Story of the Village of Le Chambon and How Goodness Happened There.* New York: HarperPerennial/HarperCollins, 1994. Hallie's book was one of the first to tell the story of Le Chambon.

Henry, Patrick. "Banishing the Coercion of Despair: Le Chambon-sur-Lignon and the Holocaust Today." *Shofar* 20, no. 2 (Winter 2001): 69–84. This article includes an insightful discussion of the rescue effort in Le Chambon and the reasons it happened there.

———. "Daniel's Choice: Daniel Trocmé (1912–1944)." *The French Review* 74, no. 4 (March 2001): 728–739. Daniel Trocmé was one of the few people from Le Chambon to perish at the hands of the Nazis.

———. "Madeleine Dreyfus, Jewish Activity, Righteous Jews." *Logos* 7, no. 1 (Winter 2004): 134–146. Madeleine Dreyfus, a member of OSE, placed refugee children with families in and around Le Chambon. Arrested by the Nazis, she survived eleven months in Bergen-Belsen.

Rittner, Carol, and Sondra Myers, eds. *The Courage to Care: Rescuers of Jews During the Holocaust.* New York: New York University Press, 1986. There are many references to Le Chambon in this book, as well as some accounts by several of Le Chambon's hidden children.

Films:

Le Chambon: La Colline aux Mille Enfants. VHS. Directed by Jean-Louis Lorenzi. Worcester, Pa.: Gateway Films, 1994. This award-winning film, directed by Jean-Louis Lorenzi, is a fictionalized account of the events at Le Chambon. It is in French with subtitles.

Weapons of the Spirit: The Astonishing Story of a Unique Conspiracy of Goodness. VHS. Directed by Pierre Sauvage. Los Angeles: Friends of Le Chambon Foundation, 1989. This documentary film was made by Pierre Sauvage, who was born in Le Chambon in 1944, while his parents were living there as refugees. The film includes interviews with some of the Chambonais who sheltered refugees as well as interviews with people who were hidden in Le Chambon. This documentary tells the story of what happened there and explores the reasons why. There is also a school version of the film available, which is thirty-five minutes in length. The video can be purchased at www.chambon.org.

BOOKS ON THE HOLOCAUST

For children and teenagers:

Gilbert, Martin. *The Routledge Atlas of the Holocaust,* 3rd ed. London and New York: Routledge, 2002. This book provides a broad overview of the Holocaust, including many maps.

Rogasky, Barbara. *Smoke and Ashes: The Story of the Holocaust,* Revised and expanded ed. New York: Holiday House, 2002. This is a book on the Holocaust for preteens and teenagers.

For adults:

Harran, Marilyn, et al. *The Holocaust Chronicle: A History in Words and Pictures.* Lincolnwood, Ill.: Publications International, Ltd., 2002. This book is a comprehensive overview of the Holocaust, which includes a detailed time line and two thousand photographs.

BIBLIOGRAPHY

Appel, Rudy. Interviewed by Deborah Durland DeSaix and Karen Gray Ruelle. Tape recording. October 24, 2002. New York, New York.

Atlas, Joseph. Interviewed by D.D.D. and K.G.R. Tape recording. November 14, 2002. Paris, France.

d'Aubigné, Jeanne Merle and Violette Mouchon, eds. Assisted by Emile C. Fabre. *Les Clandestins de Dieu: CIMADE 1939–1945.* Geneva, Switzerland: Editions Labor et Fides, 1989.

Barraud, Gabrielle. Interviewed by D.D.D. and K.G.R. Tape recording. April 6, 2004. Le Chambon-sur-Lignon, France.

Bernstein, Erna Heymann. Unpublished autobiographical piece by Erna Heymann Bernstein. 2003.

Bernstein, Erna Heymann. Interviewed by D.D.D. and K.G.R. via telephone. 2004.

Bohny, August. Interviewed by D.D.D. and K.G.R. Tape recording. November 9, 2002. Basel, Switzerland.

Bohny-Reiter, Friedel. *Journal de Rivesaltes 1941–1942.* Translated from original German into French by Michèle Fleury-Seemüller. Carouge-Genève, Switzerland: Editions Zoé, 1993.

Bollon, Gérard. Interviewed by D.D.D. and K.G.R. Tape recording. November 12, 2002, and April 5, 2004. Le Chambon-sur-Lignon, France.

———. "Contribution à l'histoire du Chambon-sur-Lignon: Le foyer universitaire des Roches et la rafle de 1943." *Cahiers de la Haute-Loire* (1996): 9–16.

———. "Identité du plateau protestant Vivarais-Lignon." *Les Cahiers du Mézenc,* no. 11 (July 1999).

———. "La Montagne protestante, terre d'accueil et de résistance pendant la seconde guerre mondiale (1939–1945)." *Les Cahiers du Mézenc,* no. 14 (July 2002): 25–32.

———. "Parcours de la Memoire." Unpublished handout loaned by Gérard Bollon.

Chave, Léon. Chart of Le Chambon Scout troops. Unpublished chart loaned by Léon Chave.

———. "Le Plateau 1940/45: Eléments de Chronologie." Unpublished article loaned by Léon Chave.

Chave, Léon, and Marthe Chave. Interviewed by D.D.D. and K.G.R. Tape recording. November 11, 2002, and April 5, 2004. Le Chambon-sur-Lignon, France.

Exposition: The Plateau Vivarais-Lignon 1939–1944: Rescue and Resistance. Exposition text from exhibit on display in Le Chambon-sur-Lignon from 1998 through present.

Fayol, Pierre. *Le Chambon-sur-Lignon sous L'Occupation 1940–1944—les résistances locales, l'aide interalliée, l'action de Virginia Hall (O.S.S.).* Paris: Edition L'Harmattan, 1990.

Feigl, Peter. Interviewed by D.D.D. and K.G.R. Tape recording. May 4, 2003. Palm City, Florida.

Fink, Paulette. Interview. Wentworth Films, Inc. Washington, D.C. United States Holocaust Memorial Museum archives. Transcript of videotaped interview #RG-50.042*0011.

Flaud, Annik. Interviewed by D.D.D. and K.G.R. Tape recording. November 11, 2002. Le Chambon-sur-Lignon, France.

Fogelman, Eva. *Conscience & Courage: Rescuers of Jews During the Holocaust.* New York: Anchor Books/Random House, 1995.

Greenfeld, Howard. *After the Holocaust.* New York: Greenwillow Books, 2001.

———. *The Hidden Children.* New York: Ticknor and Fields, 1993.

Hallie, Philip. *Lest Innocent Blood Be Shed: The Story of the Village of Le Chambon and How Goodness Happened There.* New York: HarperPerennial/HarperCollins, 1994.

Harran, Marilyn, et al. *The Holocaust Chronicle: A History in Words and Pictures.* Lincolnwood, Ill.: Publications International, Ltd., 2002.

Henry, Patrick. "Banishing the Coercion of Despair: Le Chambon-sur-Lignon and the Holocaust Today." *Shofar* 20, no. 2 (Winter 2001): 69–84.

———. "Daniel's Choice: Daniel Trocmé (1912–1944)." *The French Review* 74, no. 4 (March 2001): 728–739.

———. "Madeleine Dreyfus, Jewish Activity, Righteous Jews." *Logos* 7, no. 1 (Winter 2004): 134–146.

Kadlecek, Jo. "Spy Code-Named 'Diane' Set Up Sabotage and Guerilla Action Against Nazis." Barnard News Archive of Barnard College, New York (2004). http://www.barnard.edu/newnews/news122104b.html

Klarsfeld, Serge. *French Children of the Holocaust: A Memorial.* New York: New York Univerity Press, 1996.

Koenig, Elisabeth. Interviewed by D.D.D. and K.G.R. Tape recording. October 3, 2002. Alexandria, Virginia.

———. Interviewed by Linda Kuzmack. January 29, 1990. United States Holocaust Memorial Museum. Transcript of taped interview #RG-50.030*111.

———. Unpublished autobiographical piece loaned by Elisabeth Koenig.

Kohn, Marguerite. "Au Flachet." *Mémoires de Mme Marguerite Kohn.* Self-published, 1995.

Kustanowitz, Esther. *The Hidden Children of the Holocaust: Teens Who Hid from the Nazis.* New York: Rosen Publishing Group, 1999.

Lazare, Lucien. *Dictionnaire des Justes de France.* Jerusalem: Yad Vashem and Paris: Editions Fayard, 2003.

———. *Rescue as Resistance: How Jewish Organizations Fought the Holocaust in France.* New York: Columbia University Press, 1996.

Lewin, Jack. Interviewed by D.D.D. and K.G.R. February 22, 2003 and May 20, 2003. Bayside, New York, and New York, New York.

Liebmann, Hanne. Interviewed by D.D.D. and K.G.R. February 22, 2003. Bayside, New York.

Liebmann, Max. Interviewed by D.D.D. and K.G.R. February 22, 2003. Bayside, New York.

Liebmann, Max K. "Odyssee to Switzerland." *The Holocaust: Personal Accounts.* Burlington: University of Vermont, 2001.

Marks, Jane. *The Hidden Children: The Secret Survivors of the Holocaust.* New York: Fawcett Columbine, 1993.

Martinon, Lise-Hélène Meyer. "Ames petits enfants." Unpublished autobiographical piece.

McClelland, Roswell. "An Unpublished Chapter in the History of the Deportation of Foreign Jews from France in 1942." Unpublished, United States Holocaust Memorial Museum archives, Washington, D.C.

Mégard, Jacqueline. Interviewed by D.D.D. and K.G.R. April 9, 2004. Etival, France.

Milgram, Claude. Interviewed by D.D.D. and K.G.R. Tape recording. April 8, 2004. Marseille, France.

Morsel, Henri. Interviewed by D.D.D. and K.G.R. Tape recording. April 7, 2004. Oppedette, France.

Nallet, Jean. Interviewed by D.D.D. and K.G.R. Tape recording. November 14, 2002. Paris, France.

Le Plateau Vivarais-Lignon Accueil et Résistance 1939–1944: Actes du Colloque du Chambon-sur-Lignon. Le Chambon-sur-Lignon: Société d'Histoire de la Montagne, 1992.

Ringle, Ken. "Trail to Le Chambon: World War II Survivor Elizabeth Koenig's Remarkable Journey." *The Washington Post* (January 19, 1990).

Rittner, Carol, and Sondra Myers, eds. *The Courage to Care: Rescuers of Jews During the Holocaust.* New York: New York University Press, 1986.

Rivière, René. "Docteur Dora Rivière." Transcript of speech given at inauguration of school named in honor of Dora Rivière in St. Etienne, France, June 14, 1987. Loaned by René Rivière.

———. Interviewed by D.D.D. and K.G.R. Tape recording. November 11, 2002, and April 6, 2004. Le Chambon-sur-Lignon, France.

Rogasky, Barbara. *Smoke and Ashes: The Story of the Holocaust.* Revised and expanded ed. New York: Holiday House, 2002.

Sauvage, Pierre. *Weapons of the Spirit: The Astonishing Story of a Unique Conspiracy of Goodness.* Friends of Le Chambon Foundation, 1989. Film.

Silver, Renée. Interviewed by D.D.D. and K.G.R. Tape recording. April 30, 2004. Garden City, New York.

"Societé d'Histoire de la Montagne, Le Plateau et L'Accueil des Juifs Réfugiés 1940–1945." Self-published pamphlet, United States Holocaust Memorial Museum archives, Washington, D.C., 1981.

Stern, Nathalie. Interviewed by D.D.D. and K.G.R. November 8, 2002, and April 3, 2004. Créteil, France.

http://www.chambon.org This is the website of the Chambon Foundation, a nonprofit organization founded by Pierre Sauvage in 1982, and incorporated in California. Mr. Sauvage was born in Le Chambon during World War II to Jewish parents who had found refuge there. His documentary film, *Weapons of the Spirit,* tells the story of rescue and refuge in Le Chambon. The Chambon Foundation is dedicated to "exploring the necessary and challenging lessons of hope intertwined with the Holocaust's unavoidable lessons of despair."

Zapruder, Alexandra, ed. *Salvaged Pages: Young Writers' Diaries of the Holocaust.* New Haven: Yale University Press, 2002.

Zeitoun, Sabine. *Ses Enfants Qu'il Fallait Sauver.* Paris: Albin Michel, 1989.

ACKNOWLEDGMENTS

WE ARE DEEPLY INDEBTED to the people who generously shared their life stories with us and welcomed us into their homes. Without them, there would be no book. A number of people helped us along on our journey, and we are truly grateful.

Annik Flaud, curator of the museum in Le Chambon-sur-Lignon (temporarily closed as of this writing), added immeasurably to our book by sharing her broad knowledge of the history and events of the plateau. She kindly read our manuscript to check for accuracy. Any errors in fact that remain are ours, not hers. Madame Flaud introduced us to Gérard Bollon, the assistant mayor of Le Chambon. His many writings on the topic of our book, as well as his meetings with us, provided much help. In addition, Madame Flaud introduced us to a number of people who spoke with us about their lives. We are indebted to her for all her help and insights.

Liza Voges and our editor, Mary Cash, were enthusiastic from the moment we talked to them about our idea for a book on Le Chambon. Mary has been a wonderful and supportive editor, and we're glad our book found a home at Holiday House.

Researching this book was like going on a treasure hunt. The New York Public Library led us to Pierre Sauvage's excellent documentary, *Weapons of the Spirit*. Mr. Sauvage led us to Pastor Trocmé's daughter, Nelly Trocmé Hewett. We're thankful to her for leading us to our first interview, with the late Elisabeth Koenig. Mrs. Hewett also put us in touch with many other people, who, in turn, led us to others.

The University of Hartford, as well as the International Center and the Hartford Art School of the University of Hartford, provided some research funding. Barbara and Edward Gray helped in numerous ways and also made our last research trip to France more delicious. Karen Martinello did a wonderful job with translations and transcriptions of interviews, all with good cheer and a generous spirit. Gary Zingher gave us inspired suggestions that helped us to shape the book.

Preston and Kitty Durland and George Inge IV were supportive right from the very beginning. George was also a valuable sounding board all along the way, and his crackerjack driving got us safely all over France and to interviews on time. Lee Ruelle gave us technical support and pitched in at home while Karen was busy writing and researching. Nina Ruelle was our first real reader and gave us the kind of useful feedback that only she could give.

And on a final note, thank goodness for chocolate! It got us through some difficult times!

PHOTO AND ART CREDITS

The photographs in this book are from the following sources and are used with permission:

Rudy Appel (private collection): pp. 12, 44, 48, 53, 54 (top & bottom), 64, 125, 156 (bottom), 170, 214, & 217

Joseph Atlas (private collection): pp. 208 & 216

Elyakim Ben-Gal (private collection): p. 18

Erna Bernstein (private collection): pp. 76 & 79

Bundesarchiv-Bildarchiv: p. 7

Chambon Foundation: pp. 16, 17 (top & bottom), 38, 42, 56, 85, 111, 136, 148, 154, 206 (bottom), 207, 238, & 241

Marthe Chave and Léon Chave (private collection): pp. 13, 106 (left & right), & 109

Deborah Durland DeSaix (private collection): p. 23

Peter Feigl (private collection): pp. 126, 137, & 141

Hanne and Max Liebmann (private collection): pp. 98, 220 (left & right), 235, & 236

Lise Martinon (private collection): pp. 150 & 156 (top)

Jacqueline Mégard (private collection): pp. 192, 194, & 195

Mémorial de la Shoah/Centre de Documentation Juive Contemporaine: pp. 60 & 68

Henri Morsel (private collection): pp. 112, 114, & 115

Jean Nallet (private collection): pp. ii, 144, & 146

Private collection: pp. 10, 15, 20, 24, 35, 58, 67, 82, 84, 88, 103, 117, 155, 158, 164, 167, 173, 174, 201, & 206 (top)

René Rivière (private collection): p. 198

Roget-Viollet Agence Photographique: p. 130

Renée Silver (private collection): pp. 178, 184, 186, &189

The United States Holocaust Memorial Museum (USHMM):

    courtesy of American Friends Service Committee: p. 8 (top)

    courtesy of American Jewish Joint Distribution Committee: p. 212

    courtesy of Amicale, France: p. 122

    courtesy of Bayerische Staatsbibliothek Müchen, p. 128

    courtesy of Friedel Bohny-Reiter: pp. 8 (bottom), 63, & 78

    courtesy of Margaret Chelnick: p. 225

    courtesy of the Collection of the Museum of Jewish Heritage—A Living Memorial to the Holocaust, New York: p. 229

    courtesy of the Franklin D. Roosevelt Library: p. 124

    courtesy of Richard Freimark: p. 2

    courtesy of Elizabeth Kaufmann Koenig: pp. 29 & 32

    courtesy of Hanna Meyer-Moses: p. 96

    courtesy of Jacob Rader Marcus Center of the American Jewish Archive: p. 52

    courtesy of National Archives and Records Administration, College Park: pp. 3, 4, 9, 46, & 223

    courtesy of Rescuers and Portraits of Moral Courage in the Holocaust: p. 41

    courtesy of Stadtarchiv Aachen: p. 91

    courtesy of Robert Trocmé: p. 204

    courtesy of YIVO Institute: p. 6

Yad Vashem (#3922/116): p. xxii

SOURCE NOTES

CHAPTER ONE **WAR! WORLD WAR II BEGINS**

Page

1   "The Final Solution" is discussed in Rogasky, *Smoke and Ashes,* p. xiii.

We found a description of Germany's economic problems in Harran, *The Holocaust Chronicle,* p. 50.

1–2   Hitler referred to Jews as maggots, etc., in his book, *Mein Kampf;* Rogasky, p. 9.

2   The Nazi view of Jews as a disease is discussed in Harran, p. 40.

Although many people were threatened by the Nazis, Jews were especially targeted, as is noted in Harran, p. 39.

2–3   The events of Kristallnacht are described in Harran, p. 144.

CHAPTER TWO **COLLABORATING WITH THE NAZIS: VICHY FRANCE**

Page

5   We learned that one needed a special pass to cross the demarcation line in Klarsfeld, *French Children of the Holocaust,* p. 4.

It took less than a week for the Vichy government to begin to pass anti-Semitic regulations, according to Klarsfeld, p. 9.

According to Klarsfeld, p. 7, the Vichy government came up with the idea of deporting Jewish children, as well as their parents, something the Nazis had not even demanded.

5–6   Klarsfeld, p. 5, delineates the dangers faced by a foreign-born Jew in France.

7   We found a description of the roundups and arrests of thousands of Jews at a time in Klarsfeld, p. 6. These roundups began in May 1941.

Klarsfeld, p. 7, describes the massive roundup of Jews taken to the Vel d'Hiv on July 16 and 17, 1942.

The brutality of the conditions under which Jews were held at the Vel d'Hiv is described in Harran, *The Holocaust Chronicle,* p. 337.

We found an official definition of death camps in Rogasky, *Smoke and Ashes,* p. xiii.

9   We were horrified to learn that many Jewish children under the age of six were

sent to their deaths by the Vichy government in Lazare, *Rescue as Resistance,* p.
172.

9   We read these devastating statistics in
Klarsfeld, p. 8.

CHAPTER THREE **AN ISOLATED HAVEN: LE CHAMBON-SUR-LIGNON
AND LA MONTAGNE PROTESTANTE**

Page

11   The persecution of the Huguenots in
France is described in Bollon, "Identité du
plateau," p. 1; Bollon, "La Montagne
protestante," p. 2; and Henry, "Banishing
the Coercion of Despair," p. 5.

12   We got our figures on the French Protestant
population from Henry, p. 4.

13   Léon and Marthe Chave described to us
the kinds of animals generally found on
farms on the plateau in our first interview
with them, pp. 2–3. The Chaves grew up
on a typical farm in the area and gave us a
great deal of information about farm life
there, pp. 2–5 and 22–23.

     Pastor Louis Comte created a program to
bring needy children to the mountains. We
found descriptions of this program in *Le
Plateau Vivarais-Lignon 1939–1944,* pp.
153–154; Bollon, p. 3; and Gabrielle
Barraud told us about it in our interview
with her, p. 1.

14   Henry highlights the close feelings of
Protestants on the plateau toward Jews and
the Jewish faith in "Banishing the
Coercion of Despair," p. 5.

     The heartwarming story of the generosity

and understanding of the Kohn
family's neighbors is told in both
Sauvage, *Weapons of the Spirit,* and
Kohn, "Au Flachet," p. 78.

We learned about Charles Guillon and
his work to help refugees in Bollon, pp.
27–28.

"The weapons of the spirit" in Sauvage.

14–15   We found the story of how Le
Chambon-sur-Lignon became a village
of refuge in Henry, p. 5.

15   In our conversations with Annik Flaud,
she described to us the large numbers
of children arriving in Le Chambon
daily.

We read about Pastor Trocmé enlisting
the help of the International Civil
Service in *Le Plateau Vivarais-Lignon
1939–1944,* p. 193.

"Action, not words" is our translation
from the original French, from *Le Plateau
Vivarais-Lignon 1939–1944,* p. 227.

15–16   The activities of the American Quakers
in the Le Chambon area are discussed
in *Exposition,* p. 9.

The contribution of the Salvation

Army to help refugee children on the plateau is discussed in *Le Plateau Vivarais-Lignon 1939–1944,* p. 205.

15–16 We learned of the role of the Fellowship of Reconciliation from conversations with and unpublished notes by Annik Flaud.

Henry details some of the charities that helped fund children's homes in Le Chambon, p. 4.

16 In our second interview with Gérard Bollon, he told us about Les Tavas and what the people there did to help the refugees.

Although it's impossible to know for sure whether every single household sheltered a refugee, many people claim that it is so. This is discussed in *Le Plateau Vivarais-Lignon 1939–1944,* p. 293.

One can find out more about the Chambon Foundation at their website, *http://www.chambon.org.*

We learned about the Coblentz family and their humorously named pig from Sauvage, *Weapons of the Spirit,* and our conversations with Annik Flaud.

19 In our interview with Peter Feigl, p. 24, he told us that as a young refugee, he found it odd that they were sent into the woods to look for mushrooms at a time of year when there wouldn't be any. As an adult, he realized it had been a ploy to keep the refugees occupied and out of danger during a raid.

Annik Flaud told us this story of the gendarmes tipping off the people they were supposed to arrest, in order to give them a chance to get away.

19–20 Oscar Osowsky speaks about making false papers in Sauvage.

20 Henry mentions the interesting fact that many years later, fleeing Jews took the same routes to freedom as did the Huguenots, p. 5.

Many of the former refugees we interviewed described their harrowing experiences crossing the border into Switzerland. There are also vivid descriptions in Pierre Piton's firsthand account of his experiences leading refugees to the border in *Le Plateau Vivarais-Lignon 1939–1944,* pp. 267 and 268.

There were joys as well as fears for many of the former refugees we interviewed. They described friendships, games, and romances.

Although French was not the first language for many of the former refugees, most of the people we interviewed told us they were able to learn French fairly quickly.

21 The Ecole Nouvelle Cévenole is described in *Exposition,* p. 16, and *Le Plateau Vivarais-Lignon 1939–1944,* p. 163.

The variety and characteristics of the teachers at the Ecole Nouvelle Cévenole are described in *Le Plateau Vivarais-Lignon 1939–1944,* pp. 161 and 163. In addition, Annik Flaud spoke to us about the school and the teachers in our conversations with her.

We read this amusing detail about the creative use of space for classrooms in *Le Plateau Vivarais-Lignon 1939–1944,* p. 166.

21   Adapting to the difficult circumstances they faced, teachers attempted to comport themselves with dignity, as an example to their students. Leaving their wooden clogs outside the classroom is one instance of this behavior, described in *Le Plateau Vivarais-Lignon 1939–1944,* p. 163.

      After our first interview with Léon and Marthe Chave, Léon gave us a chart he had made of the Le Chambon Boy Scout troops during the war, including the totem names of each troop. His totem was the Stag.

22   We saw the building that housed the Hôtel du Lignon, right next door to the building that once housed Tante Soly,

pointed out to us by Annik Flaud. We also read about their proximity in Bollon, "Parcours de la Memoire," p. 1.

Annik Flaud spoke to us about Léon Eyraud. We also learned about his involvement with the Resistance in Sauvage.

Henry describes the attitudes of the Protestants on the plateau toward the Vichy government on pp. 4–5.

The anecdote about Lamirand's visit to Le Chambon and the unwelcome reception he received is described in a number of sources, including Sauvage; *Exposition,* p. 17; and *Le Plateau Vivarais-Lignon 1939–1944,* pp. 393–394.

CHAPTER FOUR **LOST: ELISABETH**

Page

25   Elisabeth is quoted in Ringle's article, "Trail to Le Chambon," as saying that she felt terrified even at that young age, when she first saw the Nazis marching through Berlin.

26   In an interview with Linda Kuzmack, Elisabeth talks about her father losing his job; Koenig, United States Holocaust Memorial Museum, p. 2.

      Elisabeth mentions attending the Czisek Art School for young children, in Koenig, p. 1.

      The passport situation and the family's travel plan and first attempt to cross the border can be found in Koenig, p. 2.

26–27 Elisabeth talks about her fear of Dachau and the vague rumors they had heard about it at that time in Ringle.

27   The way Elisabeth's mother finally was able to obtain visas and Elisabeth's arrival in Paris are both recounted in Ringle, and Koenig, p. 3.

27–28 Elisabeth talks about her former teacher's going to teach German in Le Chambon in Koenig, p. 4.

28   Elisabeth talks about Ernest in Koenig, p. 4, and Zapruder, *Salvaged Pages,* p. 45.

      The family's precarious situation is described in Koenig, pp. 4–5.

28   Elisabeth expresses her desire to be an artist in Koenig, p. 4.

29   Elisabeth voices her concern for Ernest in her diary in Zapruder, p. 45.

      We found the amusing name Elisabeth gave to her bicycle in Koenig, p. 6.

30   Elisabeth describes the experience of her father as a *prestataire,* and what that meant in Zapruder, pp. 47–48, and Koenig, p. 6.

      Elisabeth's state of anxiety is made clear in Zapruder, pp. 49–50.

      Elisabeth expresses her anguished feelings about Ernest's safety in Zapruder, p. 54.

      Elisabeth relates what the concierge told them in Koenig, p. 7.

30–31 Elisabeth writes vividly in her diary about the stressful, chaotic way she and her mother were forced to travel, and how they determined where to meet, in Zapruder, pp. 56–60.

31–32 We learned what items Elisabeth brought with her when she fled Paris and her indignation at being thought a spy in Ringle, and Zapruder, pp. 60–61.

32   Elisabeth describes their experience of being held at the police station and their subsequent release in Zapruder, pp. 61–62.

      Elisabeth describes trying to find her mother and father in Koenig, pp. 8–9.

33   Elisabeth talks about her desperate search for her brother in Toulouse, in Koenig, p. 10.

      We read about Elisabeth's amazing

discovery of a letter from her mother in Ringle, and in Koenig, pp. 10–11.

We found the name of the town where Elisabeth's family settled in Zapruder, p. 40.

Elisabeth's former teacher found a place for her in Le Chambon, as recounted in Ringle, and Koenig, p. 14.

34   Elisabeth describes the Trocmé children and her care of them in Koenig, pp. 14–15.

      Elisabeth used this nickname for Magda Trocmé, Koenig, p. 15.

      We translated the words to this lovely song from the original French in Koenig, unpublished autobiographical piece, p. 2. When we interviewed Elisabeth, she sang it for us.

35   Elisabeth's moving account of her attempts to help the young refugees in La Guespy can be found in Koenig, United States Holocaust Memorial Museum, p. 16.

      Elisabeth talks about the particular difficulties teenagers had because of food shortages, and tells the story of the boy stealing a potato in Koenig, p. 20.

35–36 We read of Elisabeth's sudden departure from Le Chambon in Koenig, p. 16.

36   Elisabeth recounts the harrowing experience of leaving Le Chambon and getting lost in a snowstorm in Koenig, pp. 16–17.

37   "Mama Trocmé," Koenig, p. 15.

      "In the few months," Koenig, unpublished autobiographical piece, p. 3.

CHAPTER FIVE **GUIDING SPIRITS: THE PASTORS**

Page

39   We read about the pastors' sheltering refugees in their homes, and how the pastors operated in their commitment to helping the refugees in *Le Plateau Vivarais-Lignon 1939–1944*, p. 18 and pp. 68–69.

We read about how the pastors passed along information in *Exposition*, p. 8.

We found information about the codes and the necessity for them in *Le Plateau Vivarais-Lignon 1939–1944*, p. 55.

We learned of the code name for Jewish refugees in *Le Plateau Vivarais-Lignon 1939–1944*, p. 225, and Sauvage, *Weapons of the Spirit*.

40   We read about how pastors would contact each other in order to find shelter for Jewish refugees in *Le Plateau Vivarais-Lignon 1939–1944*, pp. 225 and 425.

Pastor Bettex tells this story of rescue in *Le Plateau Vivarais-Lignon 1939–1944*, p. 69.

Pastor Delizy tells of his clandestine radio activity in *Le Plateau Vivarais-Lignon 1939–1944*, p. 74.

Pastor Curtet recounts his experiences helping the refugees in *Le Plateau Vivarais-Lignon 1939–1944*, p. 56–57.

40–41   Pastor Besson describes his parish and hiding refugees in *Le Plateau Vivarais-Lignon 1939–1944*, pp. 75–76.

42   Pastor Morel's activities during the Occupation are described in *Le Plateau Vivarais-Lignon 1939–1944*, pp. 611–613.

42–43   This is our translation from the original French of a quotation by former Le Chambon student George Menut, attributed by him to Pastor Trocmé, from *Le Plateau Vivarais-Lignon 1939–1944*, p. 395.

43   We found a description of Pastor Trocmé's adamant defense of the refugees in *Le Plateau Vivarais-Lignon 1939–1944*, p. 395.

We learned of many of the things Roger Darcissac did during the war to protect refugees in Lazare, *Dictionnaire des Justes de France*, p. 198. *Le Plateau Vivarais-Lignon 1939–1944*, p. 371, indicates the importance of the two pastors and Darcissac to the rescue effort.

We learned of Pastors Trocmé and Theis going into hiding near the end of the war in *Plateau Vivarais-Lignon 1939–1944*, pp. 383 and 398; in Lazare, p. 545; and from our conversations with Annik Flaud.

CHAPTER SEVEN **ONE BIG FAMILY: SWISS AID FOR CHILDREN AND AUGUST BOHNY**

Page

57 August Bohny describes setting up a farm school in *Le Plateau Vivarais-Lignon 1939–1944,* p. 193, and in our interview with him, p. 5.

57–58 Bohny describes the carpentry workshop in *Le Plateau Vivarais-Lignon 1939–1944,* p. 212.

58 This estimate of the number of children cared for in the Swiss Aid homes comes directly from Bohny, in our interview with him, p. 5.

59 We found statistics on the number of students in each of the Swiss Aid houses in *Le Plateau Vivarais-Lignon 1939–1944,* pp. 290–291.

Bohny tells the story of their travails finding enough milk for all the children in *Le Plateau Vivarais-Lignon 1939–1944,* p. 196.

In our interview with Bohny, p. 7, he told us about getting to know the shopkeepers while he helped out at the temple, and their generosity.

In our first interview with Nathalie Stern, p. 13, she told us about clothing being passed down from child to child.

Bohny talks about the difficulties of keeping the children in decent shoes in *Le Plateau Vivarais-Lignon 1939–1944,* p. 197.

Bohny told us about the loving routine he insisted on for the children each evening in our interview with him, p. 18.

60 "The children knew" is our translation of the original French from our interview with Bohny, p. 9.

Bohny described to us Pastor Trocmé's storytelling talents in our interview with him, p. 13.

60–61 Bohny described to us the warning signals they used among the Swiss Aid houses in our interview with him, p. 10.

61 We found the ages of children who stayed at the Swiss Aid homes in *Le Plateau Vivarais-Lignon 1939–1944,* pp. 290–291.

Bohny recounts the story of what happened when the gendarmes tried to arrest teenagers in his care in *Le Plateau Vivarais-Lignon 1939–1944,* pp. 200–201.

In our interview with Bohny, p. 11, he told us about what happened when he tried to retrieve the girl who was hiding on the farm.

62 We heard the story of how he helped the Resistance in our interview with Bohny, p. 12.

Chapter Ten Escape to Switzerland

Page

83   We read about Mireille Philip's nickname and the clever use of her sewing basket in a firsthand account by Pastor Bettex, in *Le Plateau Vivarais-Lignon 1939–1944,* p. 69.

83–84 We learned of Philip's unconventional disguise in discussions with Annik Flaud and in *Le Plateau Vivarais-Lignon 1939–1944,* p. 383.

84   In our interview with Jack Lewin, he told us about watching Pastor Theis make his false identity card.

86   Pierre Piton describes his perilous travels leading refugees to safety and his two arrests by the police in *Le Plateau Vivarais-Lignon 1939–1944,* pp. 262–270.

In our discussions with Annik Flaud, she recounted the many ways refugees crossed into Switzerland.

We learned about Charles Guillon's work helping refugees in Bollon, "La Montagne protestante," p. 28.

86–87 Pastor Donadille tells the story of the police raid and the woman's trick in *Le Plateau Vivarais-Lignon 1939–1944,* pp. 185–186.

87   Pastor Donadille also writes about the fate of the little girl in *Le Plateau Vivarais-Lignon 1939–1944,* p. 187.

Chapter Twelve Spies Next Door: Léon and Marthe

Page

108   Marthe Chave described her *sabots* to us in our first interview with her and Léon, p. 6.

110   Annik Flaud told us about Bubi's mother teaching Lydie how to sew.

Chapter Fourteen Spies and Fighters: The Resistance and the Maquis

Page

124 We learned about the Resistance's trying to sway Russian soldiers from *Exposition,* p. 26, and our discussions with Annik Flaud.

Both René Rivière and Gabrielle Barraud told us about the secrecy of the members of the Resistance, in our second interview with Rivière, pp. 18–19, and our interview with Barraud, p. 5.

125 We read about Pastor Theis's rule for the Ecole Nouvelle Cévenole in *Le Plateau Vivarais-Lignon 1939–1944,* p. 168.

We learned some of Virginia Hall's aliases in our first interview with Léon and Marthe Chave, p. 31, and our interview with Jean Nallet, p. 2.

We learned many details about Virginia Hall from Kadlecek, "Spy Code-Named 'Diane.'"

Chapter Fifteen Sabotaging the Nazis: Peter

Page

134 In an excerpt from Peter's diary, he writes of his fear of being arrested in spite of the official telegram giving him permission to leave France, and his concern for his parents, Zapruder, *Salvaged Pages,* p. 71.

135 Peter writes often of his parents in his diary, Zapruder, p. 73.

In his diary, Peter describes how he came to be sent to Le Chambon, Zapruder, pp. 77–78.

135–136 His arrival in Le Chambon and his settling in are described by Peter in his diary, Zapruder, p. 78.

138 Peter details some of the Resistance activities in his diary excerpts, Zapruder, p. 79.

139 Amidst everyday observations about classmates and school, Peter mentions an air raid in his diary, Zapruder, p. 85.

Peter writes in his diary about the German army and the order to report to the gendarmerie, Zapruder, p. 87.

140–142 Peter describes his crossing into Switzerland in Zapruder, p. 88.

Chapter Sixteen IN THE MAQUIS: JEAN

Page

149 Some of the details about Jean's
relationship with the Meyer family and
what they did for him come from

unpublished notes by Lise Meyer
Martinon, p. 8.

Chapter Seventeen A BRIGHT SPIRIT: LISE

Page

153–154 We learned from Bollon, "Parcours de
la Memoire," p. 1, that most of the
children at Tante Soly were Jewish.

Chapter Eighteen HOUSE OF REFUGE AND RESISTANCE: GABRIELLE

Page

162 "I made blood pudding" is our
translation from the original French,
from our interview with Gabrielle
Barraud, p. 11.

162–163 We read in Lazare, *Dictionnaire des*

Justes de France, p. 70, the date that
Yad Vashem awarded to Gabrielle
Barraud and her mother the title
"Righteous Among the Nations."

Chapter Nineteen HIDING CHILDREN: OSE AND MADELEINE DREYFUS

Page

165 Both *Le Plateau Vivarais-Lignon
1939–1944,* p. 223, and Henry,
"Madeleine Dreyfus," p. 134, describe
how Madeleine Dreyfus began
working with OSE, hiding Jewish
children on the plateau.

We learned about how Dreyfus

prepared the children for their journey
in *Le Plateau Vivarais-Lignon
1939–1944,* p. 224; Henry,
"Madeleine Dreyfus," p. 135; and from
our discussions with Annik Flaud.

In our conversations with Annik Flaud,
and in *Le Plateau Vivarais-Lignon*

1939–1944, pp. 217–218, we learned that Madame Déléage, or, more often, her daughter, would usually meet the children as they disembarked in Le Chambon.

166   Dreyfus remembers Madame Déléage telling her this story, complete with gestures, about defying the Gestapo in *Le Plateau Vivarais-Lignon 1939–1944,* p. 218.

"We didn't find any Jews" is our translation from the original French, from *Le Plateau Vivarais-Lignon 1939–1944,* p. 218.

We learned of the many things Dreyfus did to help the young refugees she had hidden in the Le Chambon area in *Le Plateau Vivarais-Lignon 1939–1944,* pp. 219 and 225, and Henry, p. 135.

166–168   This touching story about the love the Francs felt toward Pierre is related in Lazarre, *Dictionnaire des Justes de France,* p. 263. Both quotes are our translations from the original French.

168   Dreyfus made these observations about the farmers and the "chores" they assigned to the children in *Le Plateau Vivarais-Lignon 1939–1944,* p. 219.

In our talks with Annik Flaud, we discussed the reserved nature of many of the people on the plateau.

We read Dreyfus's account of the story of the two teenage boys in *Le Plateau Vivarais-Lignon 1939–1944,* p. 218. The quote is our translation from the original French. She also recounted the story in Sauvage, *Weapons of the Spirit.*

We read about Dreyfus's sons in her account in *Le Plateau Vivarais-Lignon 1939–1944,* p. 219. The quote is our translation from the original French.

168–169   We learned that Dreyfus was sent to Bergen-Belsen in Henry, "Madeleine Dreyfus," p. 136.

169   Dreyfus's fate is related in *Le Plateau Vivarais-Lignon 1939–1944,* pp. 219 and 226, and Henry, p. 137.

CHAPTER TWENTY **TWO LOVING FAMILIES: CLAUDE**

Page

173   We read about the Olliviers giving Claude the name "Claudie" in Lazare, *Dictionnaire des Justes de France,* p. 434.

CHAPTER TWENTY-THREE **A FAMILY IN THE RESISTANCE: RENÉ**

Page

202   We learned about Dora Rivière from her nephew's speech about her, Rivière, "Docteur Dora Rivière," and from *Le Plateau Vivarais-Lignon 1939–1944,* p. 73.

In Pierre Piton's account in *Le Plateau Vivarais-Lignon 1939–1944,* p. 266, we read about how René's father participated in helping refugees who were fleeing to Switzerland.

202–203   We learned that René's father had to hide for a while at the home of the Dolmazon family, in *Le Plateau Vivarais-Lignon 1939–1944,* pp. 73–74.

CHAPTER TWENTY-FOUR **TRAGEDY: DANIEL TROCMÉ AND LA MAISON DES ROCHES**

Page

205   "For me, Le Chambon" is our translation from the original French of part of Daniel Trocmé's letter of Sept. 11, 1942, from Bollon, "Contribution à l'histoire," p. 4.

We learned of the ages of the children in Les Grillons in *Le Plateau Vivarais-Lignon 1939–1944,* p. 291.

A letter from Daniel Trocmé is excerpted in Bollon, p. 4. In it, he writes about having to clothe the children in his care from head to toe.

We read about Daniel Trocmé supplying the children in his care with false papers in Henry, "Daniel's Choice," p. 733.

A letter from Daniel Trocmé is excerpted in Bollon, p. 4. In it he mentions getting *sabots* for the children.

In our interview with Peter Feigl, p. 23, he described the disdain he had for the sandals Daniel Trocmé made out of tires for the children at Les Grillons.

206   In Bollon, "Contribution à l'histoire," pp. 25–29, we learned of the origins of the students at La Maison des Roches; and in Bollon, "Parcours de la Memoire," p. 4, we discovered how many of them were Jewish.

206–207   We learned of the fate of the students who were arrested at La Maison des Roches from *Exposition,* p. 19, and Henry, p. 730.

207   We read of Daniel Trocmé's continuing concern for the children who had been in his care in Henry, pp. 736–737.

"How is each" is our translation from the original French of part of Daniel Trocmé's letter of Sept. 23, 1943, in Henry, p. 737.

"My greatest joy" is our translation from the original French of part of Daniel Trocmé's letter of Sept. 12, 1943, in Henry, pp. 737–738.

We learned of Daniel Trocmé's ultimate fate in Henry, p. 736.

Chapter Twenty-six **Love in Wartime: Hanne and Max**

Epilogue

Postscript

Page

243   In our discussions with Annik Flaud, she told us about the many people on the plateau who had received Yad Vashem's "Righteous Among the Nations" medal. She showed us the award received by Le Chambon and the surrounding communities, which now hangs in the Town Hall of Le Chambon. We found all of the specific information in Lazare, *Dictionnaire des Justes de France.*

INDEX

Page numbers in *italics* refer to illustrations.